SRA
Open Court Reading

Book 1

Friendship

•

City Wildlife

•

Imagination

SRA Open Court Reading

Book 1

Program Authors
Carl Bereiter
Marilyn Jager Adams
Marlene Scardamalia
Robbie Case
Anne McKeough
Michael Pressley
Marsha Roit
Jan Hirshberg
Ann Brown
Joe Campione
Iva Carruthers
Gerald H. Treadway, Jr.

SRA

A Division of The McGraw·Hill Companies

Columbus, Ohio

Acknowledgments

Grateful acknowledgment is given to the following publishers and copyright owners for permissions granted to reprint selections from their publications. All possible care has been taken to trace ownership and secure permission for each selection included.

Curtis Brown, Ltd.: **Copyright © 1970 by Phyllis Busch. Excerpt from CITY LOTS: LIVING THINGS IN VACANT SPOTS, published by World Publishing Co. Reprinted by permission of Curtis Brown, Ltd. "How Dog Outwitted Leopard" by Verna Aardema. Copyright © 1960 by Verna Aardema. First appeared in TALES FROM THE STORY HAT, published by Coward McCann. Reprinted by permission of Curtis Brown, Ltd.**

Children's Press, Inc.: PICASSO, written and illustrated by Mike Venezia. Copyright © 1988 by Children's Press, Inc. Reprinted with permission of Children's Press, Inc., Chicago.

Children's Television Workshop: "City Critters: Wild Animals Live in Cities, Too" by Richard Chevat from the September 1988 issue of "3-2-1 Contact Magazine." Copyright 1988 Children's Television Workshop (New York, New York). All rights reserved.

Dutton Children's Books, a division of Penguin Putnam Inc.: THE BOY WHO DIDN'T BELIEVE IN SPRING by Lucille Clifton. Copyright © 1973 by Lucille Clifton, text. Used by permission of Dutton Children's Books, a division of Penguin Putnam Inc. "The Sun is a Yellow-Tipped Porcupine," from WHIRLWIND IS A GHOST DANCING by Natalia Belting. Copyright © 1974 by Natalia Belting. Used by permission of Dutton Children's Books, a division of Penguin Putnam Inc.

Lois L. Fax: "How Dog Outwitted Leopard" from TALES FROM THE STORY HAT by Verna Aardema, illustrations by Elton Fax. Illustrations copyright © 1995 by the Estate of Elton Fax. Reprinted with permission of Lois L. Jones-Fax, Betty Ward and Leon Speaks.

Greenwillow Books, a division of William Morrow & Company, Inc.: "Priscilla, Meet Felicity" from BEST ENEMIES by Kathleen Leverich. Text copyright © 1989 by Kathleen Leverich. By permission of Greenwillow Books, a division of William Morrow & Company, Inc..

Harcourt Brace & Company: "Fog" from CHICAGO POEMS by Carl Sandburg, copyright © 1916 by Holt, Rinehart and Winston and renewed 1944 by Carl Sandburg, reprinted by permission of Harcourt Brace & Company. "Raccoon" from THE LLAMA WHO HAD NO PAJAMA: 100 FAVORITE POEMS, copyright © 1973 by Mary Ann Hoberman, reprinted by permission of Harcourt Brace & Company. TEAMMATES by Peter Golenbock, text copyright © 1990 by Golenbock Communications, illustrations copyright © 1990 by Paul Bacon, reproduced by permission of Harcourt Brace & Company.

HarperCollins Publishers: JANEY by CHARLOTTE ZOLOTOW. COPYRIGHT © 1973 BY CHARLOTTE ZOLOTOW. Used by permission of HarperCollins Publishers. STEVIE by JOHN STEPTOE. COPYRIGHT © 1969 BY JOHN L. STEPTOE. USED BY PERMISSION OF HARPERCOLLINS PUBLISHERS AND THE ESTATE OF JOHN L. STEPTOE. Used by permission of HarperCollins Publishers WITH THE APPROVAL OF THE ESTATE OF JOHN L. STEPTOE. THROUGH GRANDPA'S EYES by PATRICIA MACLACHLAN, illustrations by DEBORAH KOGAN RAY. TEXT COPYRIGHT © 1980 BY PATRICIA MACLACHLAN. ILLUSTRATIONS COPYRIGHT © 1980 BY DEBORAH KOGAN RAY. Used by permission of HarperCollins Publishers.

Trina Schart Hyman: "The Tree House" from THE BIG BOOK OF PEACE by Lois Lowry, illustrations by Trina Schart Hyman. Illustrations copyright © 1991 by Trina Schart Hyman. Reprinted with permission of Trina Schart Hyman.

Little, Brown and Company: From URBAN ROOSTS by Barbara Bash. Copyright © 1990 by Barbara Bash. By permission of Little, Brown and Company.

Lothrop, Lee & Shepard Books, a division of William Morrow & Company, Inc.: "The Apple" from EATS by Arnold Adoff. Text copyright © 1979 by Arnold Adoff. By permission of Lothrop, Lee & Shepard Books, a division of William Morrow & Company, Inc.. ROXABOXEN by Alice McLerran. Illustrated by Barbara Cooney. Text copyright © 1991 by Alice McLerran. Illustrations copyright © 1991 by Barbara Cooney. By permission of Lothrop, Lee & Shepard Books, a division of William Morrow & Company, Inc..

Margaret K. McElderry Books, an imprint of Simon & Schuster Children's Publishing Division: "The Cat Who Became a Poet" by Margaret Mahy, illustrated by Quentin Blake. Reprinted with the permission of Margaret K. McElderry Books, an imprint of Simon & Schuster Children's Publishing Division from NONSTOP NONSENSE by Margaret Mahy, illustrated by Quentin Blake. Text copyright © 1977 Margaret Mahy. Illustrations copyright © 1977 Quentin Blake.

Harold Ober Associates Incorporated: "The Tree House" from THE BIG BOOK OF PEACE by Lois Lowry. Reprinted by permission of Harold Ober Associates Incorporated. **Copyright © 1990 by Lois Lowry.**

Oberon Press: "The Worm" is reprinted from *Collected Poems of Raymond Souster* by permission of Oberon Press.

The Orion Publishing Group Ltd.: "The Cat Who Became a Poet" from NONSTOP NONSENSE by Margaret Mahy, illustrations by Quentin Blake. Text copyright © 1977 by Margaret Mahy. Illustrations copyright © 1977 by Quentin Blake. Reprinted with permission of The Orion Publishing Group Ltd.

Pantheon Books, a division of Random House, Inc.: "Gloria Who Might Be My Best Friend" from STORIES JULIAN TELLS by Ann Cameron, illustrated by Ann Strugnell. Text copyright © 1981 by Ann Cameron. Illustrations copyright © 1981 by Ann Strugnell. Reprinted by permission of Pantheon Books, a division of Random House, Inc.

Marian Reiner: "Houses" from UP THE WINDY HILL by Aileen Fisher. Copyright ©1953 by Abelard Press. © renewed 1981 by Aileen Fisher. Reprinted by permission of Marian Reiner for the author. "Pigeons" from I THOUGHT I HEARD THE CITY by Lilian Moore. Copyright © 1969 Lilian Moore. © renewed 1997 Lilian Moore Reavin. Reprinted by permission of Marian Reiner for the author.

Simon & Schuster Books for Young Readers, Simon & Schuster Children's Publishing Division: **THE BREMEN TOWN MUSICIANS by the Bros. Grimm, illustrated by Joseph Paleček. *Text and illustrations copyright © 1988 by Verlag Neugebauer Press, Salzburg, Austria.*** Reprinted with permission of Simon & Schuster Books for Young Readers, Simon & Schuster Children's Publishing Division. All rights reserved. **SUNFLOWERS FOR TINA by Anne Baldwin, illustrated by Ann Grifalconi. *Text copyright © 1970 by Anne Baldwin. Illustrations copyright © 1970 by Ann Grifalconi.*** Reprinted with permission of Simon & Schuster Books for Young Readers, Simon & Schuster Children's Publishing Division. All rights reserved.

Steck-Vaughn Company: ANGEL CHILD, DRAGON CHILD by Michele Maria Surat, illustrations by Vo-Dinh Mai. Copyright © 1983 by Raintree/Steck-Vaughn Publishers. Reprinted with permission of Steck-Vaughn Companys.

Viking Children's Books, a division of Penguin Putnam Inc.: MAKE WAY FOR DUCKLINGS by Robert McCloskey. Copyright © 1941 by Robert McCloskey, renewed © 1969 by Robert McCloskey. Used by permission of Viking Children's Books, a division of Penguin Putnam Inc.

WGBH Educational Foundation: "City Superheroes" from THE CITY KID'S FIELD GUIDE by Ethan Herberman. Copyright © 1989 by Ethan Herberman. Reprinted with permission of WGHB Educational Foundation.

SRA/McGraw-Hill

A Division of The **McGraw·Hill** Companies

Copyright © 2000 by SRA/McGraw-Hill.

Send all inquiries to:
SRA/McGraw-Hill
8787 Orion Place
Columbus, Ohio 43240

Printed in the United States of America.

ISBN 0-02-830954-5

6 7 8 9 VHP 04 03 02 01

Program Authors

Carl Bereiter, Ph.D.
University of Toronto

Marilyn Jager Adams, Ph.D.
BBN Technologies

Michael Pressley, Ph.D.
University of Notre Dame

Marsha Roit, Ph.D.
National Reading Consultant

Robbie Case, Ph.D.
University of Toronto

Anne McKeough, Ph.D.
University of Toronto

Jan Hirshberg, Ed.D.

Marlene Scardamalia, Ph.D.
University of Toronto

Ann Brown, Ph.D.
University of California at Berkeley

Joe Campione, Ph.D.
University of California at Berkeley

Iva Carruthers, Ph.D.
Northeastern Illinois University

Gerald H. Treadway, Jr., Ed.D.
San Diego State University

Table *of* Contents

UNIT 1

Friendship 12

Gloria Who Might Be My Best Friend 14
from **The Stories Julian Tells**
realistic fiction by Ann Cameron
illustrated by Ann Strugnell
Meet the Author, Ann Cameron
Meet the Illustrator, Ann Strugnell 26
Theme Connections 27
  Irma Simonton Black Award

Angel Child, Dragon Child 28
realistic fiction by Michele Maria Surat
illustrated by Vo-Dinh Mai
Meet the Author, Michele Maria Surat
Meet the Illustrator, Vo-Dinh Mai 44
Theme Connections 45
  ALA Booklist Editor's Choice

Stevie 46
realistic fiction written and
illustrated by John Steptoe
Meet the Author/Illustrator, John Steptoe 56
Theme Connections 57
  ALSC Notable Children's Book

Janey 58
a poem by Charlotte Zolotow
illustrated by Leah Palmer Preiss

Priscilla, Meet Felicity 60
from **Best Enemies**

realistic fiction by Kathleen Leverich
illustrated by Len Ebert

Meet the Author, Kathleen Leverich

Meet the Illustrator, Len Ebert 82

Theme Connections 83

FINE Art 84

Conjunction. Romare Bearden
Children Had Few Toys. William Barnhill
The Good Friends. Honoré Daumier

The Tree House 86

realistic fiction by Lois Lowry
illustrated by Trina Schart Hyman

Meet the Author, Lois Lowry

Meet the Illustrator, Trina Schart Hyman 98

Theme Connections 99

How Dog Outwitted Leopard 100

from *Tales from the Story Hat*
an African folktale retold by Verna Aardema
illustrated by Elton Fax

Meet the Author, Verna Aardema

Meet the Illustrator, Elton Fax 106

Theme Connections 107

Teammates 108

a biography by Peter Golenbock
illustrated by Paul Bacon

Meet the Author, Peter Golenbock

Meet the Illustrator, Paul Bacon 118

Theme Connections 119

Notable Children's Trade Book (Social Studies)

Bibliography 120

Table *of* Contents

UNIT 2

City Wildlife 122

City Critters: Wild Animals Live in Cities, Too ...124
an informational text by Richard Chevat
from *3-2-1 Contact* magazine
Meet the Author, Richard Chevat 130
Theme Connections 131

City Lots: Living Things in Vacant Spots 132
from the nonfiction book by Phyllis S. Busch
illustrated by Pamela Carroll
Meet the Author, Phyllis S. Busch
Meet the Illustrator, Pamela Carroll 142
Theme Connections 143

The Boy Who Didn't Believe in Spring 144
realistic fiction by Lucille Clifton
illustrated by Brinton Turkle
Meet the Author, Lucille Clifton
Meet the Illustrator, Brinton Turkle 154
Theme Connections 155

Fine Art 156
Lunch in the Gardens. Beryl Cook
Cable Car Festival. Dong Kingman

Urban Roosts: Where Birds Nest in the City ...158
*from the nonfiction book written
and illustrated by* Barbara Bash
Meet the Author/Illustrator, Barbara Bash 172
Theme Connections 173
Outstanding Science Trade Book Award

The Worm 174
a poem by Raymond Souster
illustrated by Robert Byrd

Pigeons 175
a poem by Lilian Moore
illustrated by Robert Byrd

Make Way for Ducklings 176
a fantasy written and illustrated by Robert McCloskey
Meet the Author/Illustrator, Robert McCloskey 184
Theme Connections 185
Caldecott Medal

City Superheroes 186
from **The City Kid's Field Guide**
an informational article by Ethan Herberman
Meet the Author, Ethan Herberman 192
Theme Connections 193
Outstanding Science Trade Book for Children

Raccoon 194
a poem by Mary Ann Hoberman
illustrated by Pamela Carroll

Sunflowers for Tina 196
realistic fiction by Anne Norris Baldwin
illustrated by Ann Grifalconi
Meet the Author, Anne Norris Baldwin
Meet the Illustrator, Ann Grifalconi 210
Theme Connections 211

Bibliography 212

Table *of* Contents

UNIT 3

Imagination 214

The Blind Men and the Elephant 216
a fable retold in verse by John Godfrey Saxe
illustrated by Lane Yerkes
Meet the Author, John Godfrey Saxe
Meet the Illustrator, Lane Yerkes 218
Theme Connections 219

Through Grandpa's Eyes 220
realistic fiction by Patricia MacLachlan
illustrated by Deborah Kogan Ray
Meet the Author, Patricia MacLachlan
Meet the Illustrator, Deborah Kogan Ray 234
Theme Connections 235
Notable Children's Trade Book (Social Studies)

The Apple 236
a poem by Arnold Adoff
illustrated by Deborah Drummond

Houses 237
a poem by Aileen Fisher
illustrated by Deborah Drummond

Fog 237
a poem by Carl Sandburg
illustrated by Deborah Drummond

The Cat Who Became a Poet 238
from ***Nonstop Nonsense***
a fantasy by Margaret Mahy
illustrated by Quentin Blake
Meet the Author, Margaret Mahy
Meet the Illustrator, Quentin Blake 244

Theme Connections 245

🏅 *Parenting's Reading Magic Award*

Fine Art 246
Cow Triptych. Roy Lichtenstein
Time Transfixed. René Magritte
The Desk. David Hockney
Baird Trogon. Robert Lostutter

Picasso 248
from the biography written and illustrated
by Mike Venezia
Meet the Author, Mike Venezia 256
Theme Connections 257

Roxaboxen 258
realistic fiction by Alice McLerran
illustrated by Barbara Cooney
Meet the Author, Alice McLerran
Meet the Illustrator, Barbara Cooney 266
Theme Connections 267

🏅 *Southwest Book Award*

The sun is a yellow-tipped porcupine 268
a Crow Indian poem
illustrated by Tricia Courtney

The Bremen Town Musicians 270
a fairy tale by the Brothers Grimm
illustrated by Josef Palec̆ek
Meet the Authors, the Brothers Grimm
Meet the Illustrator, Josef Palec̆ek 278
Theme Connections 279

Bibliography 280

Writer's Handbook 282

Glossary 337

Friendship

Friendship can be confusing, nice, sad, and very, very important. What is a friend? How do you become a friend? What can you expect of a friend? Everyone has these questions, but what are the answers?

13

Gloria
Who Might Be
My Best Friend

from *The Stories Julian Tells*
by Ann Cameron
illustrated by Ann Strugnell

If you have a girl for a friend, people find out and
tease you. That's why I didn't want a girl for a
friend—not until this summer, when I met Gloria.

It happened one afternoon when I was walking
down the street by myself. My mother was visiting a
friend of hers, and Huey was visiting a friend of his.
Huey's friend is five and so I think he is too young to
play with. And there aren't any kids just my age. I was
walking down the street feeling lonely.

A block from our house I saw a moving van in front of a brown house, and men were carrying in chairs and tables and bookcases and boxes full of I don't know what. I watched for a while, and suddenly I heard a voice right behind me.

"Who are you?"

I turned around and there was a girl in a yellow dress. She looked the same age as me. She had curly hair that was braided into two pigtails with red ribbons at the ends.

"I'm Julian," I said. "Who are you?"

"I'm Gloria," she said. "I come from Newport. Do you know where Newport is?"

I wasn't sure, but I didn't tell Gloria. "It's a town on the ocean," I said.

"Right," Gloria said. "Can you turn a cartwheel?"

She turned sideways herself and did two cartwheels on the grass.

I had never tried a cartwheel before, but I tried to copy Gloria. My hands went down in the grass, my feet went up in the air, and—I fell over.

I looked at Gloria to see if she was laughing at me. If she was laughing at me, I was going to go home and forget about her.

But she just looked at me very seriously and said, "It takes practice," and then I liked her.

"I know where there's a bird's nest in your yard," I said.

"Really?" Gloria said. "There weren't any trees in the yard, or any birds, where I lived before."

I showed her where a robin lives and has eggs. Gloria stood up on a branch and looked in. The eggs were small and pale blue. The mother robin squawked at us, and she and the father robin flew around our heads.

"They want us to go away," Gloria said. She got down from the branch, and we went around to the front of the house and watched the moving men carry two rugs and a mirror inside.

"Would you like to come over to my house?" I said.

"All right," Gloria said, "if it is all right with my mother." She ran in the house and asked.

It was all right, so Gloria and I went to my house, and I showed her my room and my games and my rock collection, and then I made strawberry Kool-Aid and we sat at the kitchen table and drank it.

"You have a red mustache on your mouth," Gloria said.

"You have a red mustache on your mouth, too," I said.

Gloria giggled, and we licked off the mustaches with our tongues.

"I wish you'd live here a long time," I told Gloria.

Gloria said, "I wish I would too.

"I know the best way to make wishes," Gloria said.

"What's that?" I asked.

"First you make a kite. Do you know how to make one?"

"Yes," I said, "I know how." I know how to make good kites because my father taught me. We make them out of two crossed sticks and folded newspaper.

"All right," Gloria said, "that's the first part of making wishes that come true. So let's make a kite."

We went out into the garage and spread out sticks and newspaper and made a kite. I fastened on the kite string and went to the closet and got rags for the tail.

"Do you have some paper and two pencils?" Gloria asked. "Because now we make the wishes."

I didn't know what she was planning, but I went in the house and got pencils and paper.

"All right," Gloria said. "Every wish you want to have come true you write on a long thin piece of paper. You don't tell me your wishes, and I don't tell you mine. If you tell, your wishes don't come true. Also, if you look at the other person's wishes, your wishes don't come true."

Gloria sat down on the garage floor again and started writing her wishes. I wanted to see what they were—but I went to the other side of the garage and wrote my own wishes instead. I wrote:

1. I wish the fig tree would be the tallest in town.
2. I wish I'd be a great soccer player.
3. I wish I could ride in an airplane.
4. I wish Gloria would stay here and be my best friend.

I folded my four wishes in my fist and went over to Gloria.

"How many wishes did you make?" Gloria asked.

"Four," I said. "How many did you make?"

"Two," Gloria said.

I wondered what they were.

"Now we put the wishes on the tail of the kite," Gloria said. "Every time we tie one piece of rag on the tail, we fasten a wish in the knot. You can put yours in first."

I fastened mine in, and then Gloria fastened in hers, and we carried the kite into the yard.

"You hold the tail," I told Gloria, "and I'll pull."

We ran through the back yard with the kite, passed the garden and the fig tree, and went into the open field beyond our yard.

The kite started to rise. The tail jerked heavily like a long white snake. In a minute the kite passed the roof of my house and was climbing toward the sun.

We stood in the open field, looking up at it. I was wishing I would get my wishes.

"I know it's going to work!" Gloria said.

"How do you know?"

"When we take the kite down," Gloria told me, "there shouldn't be one wish in the tail. When the wind takes all your wishes, that's when you know it's going to work."

The kite stayed up for a long time. We both held the string. The kite looked like a tiny black spot in the sun, and my neck got stiff from looking at it.

"Shall we pull it in?" I asked.

"All right," Gloria said.

We drew the string in more and more until, like a tired bird, the kite fell at our feet.

We looked at the tail. All our wishes were gone. Probably they were still flying higher and higher in the wind.

Maybe I would get to be a good soccer player and have a ride in an airplane and the tallest fig tree in town. And Gloria would be my best friend.

"Gloria," I said, "did you wish we would be friends?"

"You're not supposed to ask me that!" Gloria said.

"I'm sorry," I answered. But inside I was smiling. I guessed one thing Gloria wished for. I was pretty sure we would be friends.

Gloria Who Might Be My Best Friend

Meet the Author

Ann Cameron was in third grade when she knew she wanted to be a writer. It has been the memories of her friends and the stories they have shared that help her write stories. She says, *"My story will never be exactly like yours. I could never tell yours for you. Your story, if it's really the way you want to tell it, can never be wrong the way an arithmetic answer is wrong; and even if your mother, your father, your teacher, or your best friend doesn't understand it, it's still right for you . . . stories are individual, special, and all different—brand new thought-flowers blooming in the garden of your head."*

Ann now lives in Guatemala, where the neighborhood children continue to inspire her writing. She is also the supervisor of a local library, where she loves to watch children read and learn.

Meet the Illustrator

Ann Strugnell is a British artist who has illustrated many children's books. She has traveled to faraway places such as Turkey, Spain, and Italy. She has even been to the United States to see New York and Cape Cod. She lives with her husband and illustrates books in the bustling city of London, England. Sometimes she comes to the United States to illustrate books as well.

Theme Connections

Think About It

The theme of this unit is Friendship. What does the story "Gloria Who Might Be My Best Friend" have to do with friendship? Here are some things you might think about:

- Both Julian and Gloria felt like they needed a friend. How might this have played a part in their friendship?
- Do you think it was hard for Julian to ask Gloria to be his friend? Why? Have you ever felt like this?
- How did the kite help them become friends?

Check the Concept/Question Board to see if there are questions there that you can answer now. If the story has raised any new questions about friendship, put the questions on the Concept/Question Board. Maybe the next story will help answer the questions.

Record Ideas

Write your personal feelings about the story in your Writing Journal. Did you think it was a good story? Why? If you didn't like the story, write about why you didn't like it. Writing in your Writing Journal can give you ideas for your own stories.

Write a Paragraph

Write a paragraph about the lesson "Gloria Who Might Be My Best Friend" taught you. Did your classmates all learn the same lesson?

Angel Child, Dragon Child

Michele Maria Surat
illustrated by Vo-Dinh Mai

My sisters skipped through the stone gate two by two. Mother was not there to skip with me. Mother was far away in Vietnam. She could not say, "Ut, my little one, be an Angel Child. Be happy in your new American school."

I hugged the wall and peeked around the corner.

A boy with fire-colored hair pointed his finger. "Pajamas!" he shouted. "They wore white pajamas to school!" The American children tilted back their long noses, laughing.

I turned away. "I want to go home to Father and Little Quang," I said.

Chi Hai's hands curved over my shoulders. "Children stay where parents place them, Ut. We stay."

Somewhere, a loud bell jangled. I lost my sisters in a swirl of rushing children. "Pa-jaa-mas!" they teased.

Inside, the children did not sit together and chant as I was taught. Instead, they waved their hands and said their lessons one by one. I hid my hands, but the teacher called my name. "Nguyen Hoa."

Hoa is my true name, but I am Ut. Ut is my at-home name—a tender name for smallest daughter.

"Hoa," the teacher said slowly. "Write your name, please." She pressed a chalk-piece to my hand and wrote in the air.

"I not understand," I whispered. The round-eyed children twittered. The red-haired boy poked my back.

"Stand up, Pajamas!"

I stood and bowed. "*Chao buoi sang,*"
I said like an Angel Child. The children
screeched like bluejays.

I sat down and flipped up my desk top, hiding
my angry Dragon face.

Deep in my pocket, I felt Mother's gift—a small
wooden matchbox with silvery edges. I took it out
and traced the *hoa-phuong* on the lid. When I
tapped the tiny drawer, Mother's eyes peeked over
the edge.

"I will keep you safe in here, Mother," I told her. "See? You will just fit beside the crayons."

Her listening face smiled. In my heart, I heard the music of her voice. "Do not be angry, my smallest daughter," she said. "Be my brave little Dragon."

So all day I was brave, even when the children whispered behind their hands and the clock needles ticked slowly. Finally, the bell trilled. Time for home!

As soon as he saw me, Little Quang crowed, "Ut! Ut! Ut!" His laughing eyes gleamed like watermelon seeds. I dropped my books and slung him on my hip.

There he rode, tugging my hair as I sorted mint leaves and chives. Little Quang strung rice noodles from the cup hooks. Father and I laughed at this happy play.

At night, small brother curled tight beside me. I showed him Mother's lonely face inside the matchbox. Together we prayed, "Keep Mother safe. Send her to us soon." With Mother's picture near, we slept like Angel Children.

In this way, many days passed.

One day at school, small feathers floated past the frosty windows. "Mother," I whispered, "this is snow. It makes everything soft, even the angry trees with no leaves to make them pretty."

My fingers danced on the desk top while I waited for the bell. When it rang, I rushed out the door.

Outside, snowflakes left wet kisses on my cheeks. "Chi Hai!" I called. "Catch some!"

"It disappears!" she cried.

Just as Chi Hai spoke, a snowrock stung her chin. That red-haired boy darted behind the dumpster. He was laughing hard.

I tried, but I could not be a noble Dragon. Before I knew it, I was scooping up snow. My hands burned and my fingers turned red. I threw my snowrock and the laughing stopped.

Suddenly, the boy tackled me! We rolled in the snow, kicking and yelling, until the principal's large hand pinched my shoulder.

"Inside!" he thundered, and he marched us to our classroom.

"We can't have this fighting. You two have to help each other," ordered the principal. He pointed at me. "Hoa, you need to speak to Raymond. Use our words. Tell him about Vietnam." Raymond glared. "And you, Raymond, you must learn to listen. You will write Hoa's story."

"But I can't understand her funny words," Raymond whined. "Anyway, I don't have a pencil."

"Use this one, then," said the principal. He slapped down a pencil, turned and slammed the door. His shoes squeegeed down the hall.

"Pajamas!" Raymond hissed. He crinkled his paper and snapped the pencil in two. He hid his head in his arms. How could I tell my story to *him*?

The clock needles blurred before my eyes. No! I *would not* be an Angel Child for this cruel-hearted boy.

But later, across the room, I heard a sniffle. Raymond's shoulders jiggled like Little Quang's when he cried for Mother.

I crept over. Gently, I tugged the sad boy's sleeve. He didn't move. "Raymond," I pleaded, "not cry. I give you cookie."

Suddenly, his head bounced up. "Hoa!" he shouted. "You said my name. You didn't use funny words." He broke off a piece of the cookie.

"I say English," I answered proudly. "And you call me Ut. Ut is my at-home name, from Vietnam."

  "Okay, *Ut*," he mumbled. "But only if you tell me what's in your matchbox."

  "My mother," I told him. We giggled and ate the cookie crumbs.

  Then Raymond asked, "Why do you need your mother's picture?"

  "Mother is far away," I said softly.

  "She didn't come with you?"

  "So many children in my family," I sighed. "No money for Mother to come."

"Wait," said Raymond. He grabbed part of the broken pencil. I handed him a new sheet of paper. "Now tell me about Vietnam," he said.

Raymond scrawled my words in black squiggles. I crayoned pictures in the margins.

When we were ready, Raymond leaned out the door. "Done!" he beamed. He waved the story like a flag.

The principal squeegeed up the hall. "You may go," said the big man.

We dashed through the stone gate together.

The next day, the principal read our story to the whole school. "These girls sailed many oceans to be here. They left behind their home, their friends, and most important of all, their mother. So now . . ."

"Ut's mother needs money for the long boat ride to America!" shouted a familiar voice. Raymond stood on his chair. "And we could have a fair and *earn* the money."

"Young man!" warned the principal.

Raymond slid down in his seat. "We could," he insisted. I hid my eyes. I held my breath. Chi Hai squeezed my hand.

"A special fair! A Vietnamese fair!" my teacher exclaimed. My eyes opened wide.

The principal's eyebrows wiggled like caterpillars. "But who will help with a Vietnamese fair?"

"Me!" cried Raymond.

"We will!" squealed the children.

"Well, what are we waiting for?" said the principal. And we all clapped for the fair.

On the special day, I wore my white *ao dai* and welcomed everyone to our Vietnamese fair. "*Chao buoi sang,*" I said, bowing like an Angel Child.

"*Chao buoi sang,*" they answered, smiling.

High above our heads, our rainbow dragon floated freely. Below, Chi Hai and her friends sold rice cakes, imperial rolls and sesame cookies. Raymond popped balloons and won three goldfish. He gave one to Little Quang. "Don't eat it," he warned.

By the end of the day, we had just enough money to send to Mother. "When will she come?" I wondered.

Every day, we walked home wondering, "When will Mother come?"

We slid through icy winter. . . .

We splish-splashed through spring rain. . . .

We tiptoed barefoot through the grass, still hoping she would come.

On the last day of school, when I knew the *hoa-phuong* were blossoming in Vietnam, Raymond and I raced home faster than all my sisters. We were the first to see Father and Little Quang at the picture window, and beside them . . .

Mother!

Angel Child, Dragon Child

Meet the Author

Michele Maria Surat teaches high school near Washington, DC, when she is not writing. The tale of Ut, the main character in this story, began when a Vietnamese student came to Surat with tear-filled eyes and shared a photograph of her mother in Vietnam. Surat wanted to tell the story of the brave students she worked with in hopes of creating an understanding between Vietnamese and American children.

Meet the Illustrator

Vo-Dinh Mai is an artist and author from Vietnam. He came to the United States when he was twenty-seven years old. Before that he spent time studying art in Paris, France. In addition to painting, Vo-Dinh loves printmaking from woodcuts. He also loves illustrating books and says, *"I believe that good illustrations can enrich the mind of a reader, young or old..."*

Vo-Dinh was back in Vietnam during the Vietnam War. He has this to say about how the war affects his art: *"If anything, the war between Vietnamese and between Vietnamese and Americans has reinforced my faith in the miracle of life."*

44

Theme Connections

Think About It

This story is something like the first story. Ut, like Gloria, has just moved to a new home. What does "Angel Child, Dragon Child" tell you about friendship? Here are some things to think about:

- Talk about how Ut is like other children in her class.
- How did Raymond and Ut get to know each other?

Check the Concept/Question Board to see if there are questions there that you can answer now. If the story has raised any new questions about friendship, put the questions on the Concept/Question Board. Maybe the next story will help answer the questions.

Record Ideas

Have you ever been the new child in school? How did you feel? Did Ut's story help you to understand how this might feel? Record your feelings in your Writing Journal.

Make a Friendship List

Write a list of things you could do to help a new student in your class feel welcome. Think about what you would like someone to do for you if you were the new student in class. Make a "Be a Friend" poster to put up in your room to remind everyone how to be a friend.

Stevie

by John Steptoe

One day my momma told me, "You know you're gonna have a little friend come stay with you."

And I said, "Who is it?"

And she said, "You know my friend Mrs. Mack? Well, she has to work all week and I'm gonna keep her little boy."

I asked, "For how long?"

She said, "He'll stay all week and his mother will come pick him up on Saturdays."

The next day the doorbell rang. It was a lady and a kid. He was smaller than me. I ran to my mother. "Is that them?"

They went in the kitchen but I stayed out in the hall to listen.

The little boy's name was Steven but his mother kept calling him Stevie. My name is Robert but my momma don't call me Robertie.

And so Steve moved in, with his old crybaby self. He always had to have his way. And he was greedy too. Everything he sees he wants. "Could I have somma that? Gimme this." Man!

Since he was littler than me, while I went to school he used to stay home and play with my toys.

47

I wished his mother would bring somma *his* toys over here to break up.

I used to get so mad at my mother when I came home after school. "Momma, can't you watch him and tell him to leave my stuff alone?"

Then he used to like to get up on my bed to look out the window and leave his dirty footprints all over my bed. And my momma never said nothin' to him.

And on Saturdays when his mother comes to pick him up, he always tries to act cute just cause his mother is there.

He picked up my airplane and I told him not to bother it. He thought I wouldn't say nothin' to him in front of his mother.

I could never go anywhere without my mother sayin' "Take Stevie with you now."

"But why I gotta take him everywhere I go?" I'd say.

"Now if you were stayin' with someone you wouldn't want them to treat you mean," my mother told me. "Why don't you and Stevie try to play nice?"

Yeah, but I always been nice to him with his old spoiled self. He's always gotta have his way anyway. I had to take him out to play with me and my friends.

"Is that your brother, Bobby?" they'd ask me.

"No."

"Is that your cousin?"

"No! He's just my friend and he's stayin' at my house and my mother made me bring him."

"Ha, ha. You gotta baby-sit! Bobby the baby-sitter!"

"Aw, be quiet. Come on, Steve. See! Why you gotta make all my friends laugh for?"

"Ha, ha. Bobby the baby-sitter," my friends said.

"Hey, come on, y'all, let's go play in the park. You comin', Bobby?" one of my friends said.

"Naw, my momma said he can't go in the park cause the last time he went he fell and hurt his knee, with his old stupid self."

And then they left.

"You see? You see! I can't even play with my friends. Man! Come on."

"I'm sorry, Robert. You don't like me, Robert? I'm sorry," Stevie said.

"Aw, be quiet. That's okay," I told him.

One time when my daddy was havin' company I was just sittin' behind the couch just listenin' to them talk and make jokes. And I wasn't makin' no noise. They didn't even know I was there!

Then here comes Stevie with his old loud self. Then when my father heard him, he yelled at *me* and told me to go upstairs.

Just cause of Stevie.

Sometimes people get on your nerves and they don't mean it or nothin' but they just bother you. Why I gotta put up with him? My momma only had one kid. I used to have a lot of fun before old stupid came to live with us.

One Saturday Steve's mother and father came to my house to pick him up like always. But they said that they were gonna move away and that Stevie wasn't gonna come back anymore.

So then he left. The next mornin' I got up to watch cartoons and I fixed two bowls of corn flakes. Then I just remembered that Stevie wasn't here.

Sometimes we had a lot of fun runnin' in and out of the house. Well, I guess my bed will stay clean from now on. But that wasn't so bad. He couldn't help it cause he was stupid.

I remember the time I ate the last piece of cake in the breadbox and blamed it on him.

We used to play Cowboys and Indians on the stoop.

I remember when I was doin' my homework I used to try to teach him what I had learned. He could write his name pretty good for his age.

I remember the time we played boogie man and we hid under the covers with Daddy's flashlight.

And that time we was playin' in the park under the bushes and we found these two dead rats and one was brown and one was black.

And him and me and my friends used to cook mickies or marshmallows in the park.

We used to have some good times together.

I think he liked my momma better than his own, cause he used to call his mother "Mother" and he called my momma "Mommy."

Aw, no! I let my corn flakes get soggy thinkin' about him.

He was a nice little guy.

He was kinda like a little brother.

Little Stevie.

Stevie

Meet the Author and Illustrator

John Steptoe began his career as an author and illustrator shortly after high school. A magazine editor recognized his talent and suggested that he "do a children's book." He used a story about his childhood that he began to write when he was sixteen. This story became the book *Stevie*. It was published in 1969 when he was only nineteen years old. If you want to read another book by John Steptoe, look for *Mufaro's Beautiful Daughters*, one of his most famous books.

Theme Connections

Think About It

What does "Stevie" tell you about friendship? Here are some things to think about:

- How were Robert and Stevie alike? How were they different?
- Do you think their age difference affected how they felt about each other? Why?
- How was this story different from the first two stories?
- What do you think about how Robert and Stevie acted?

Check the Concept/Question Board to see if there are questions there that you can answer now. If the story has raised any new questions about friendship, put the questions on the Concept/Question Board. Maybe the next story will help answer the questions.

Record Ideas

Did you like the story "Stevie?" Why or why not? Does it remind you of experiences you have had with other children or with brothers and sisters? Write about why the story reminds you of those things.

How Do Friends Behave?

Look at the story again. Write down things that Robert and Stevie each did that friends shouldn't do. With your classmates, write down things both boys could have done to help their friendship.

Janey

Charlotte Zolotow
illustrated by Leah Palmer Preiss

Janey
it's lonely
all day long
since you moved away.

When I walk in the rain
and the leaves are wet
and clinging to the sidewalk
I remember
how we used to walk
home from school
together.

I remember how you had to touch
everything we passed,
the wet leaves
of the privet hedge,
even the stucco part
of the wall.
I only look with my eyes.

I still have the pebble
you found on the
playground.
And I remember how
you skipped flat rocks
into the pond.
Mine just sank.

Sometimes when I'm playing
with the other kids
I remember how your voice sounded.
No one else sounds like you.

I remember sometimes
we both talked at once
and when we stopped
we'd said the same thing.
And I remember sitting on the steps
in the sun and not talking
at all.
There is no one else
I can sit with
and not talk.

I remember how
we'd go home for dinner
and I could hardly wait
for dinner to end
to call you.
But sometimes you called me first.

And I remember last Christmas
I half didn't want
to give you your present,
I wanted it so much myself.

You told me later
you half didn't want to give me mine
but when we each opened our present
it was the *same* book.
I think of you every time
I read the stories over again.

When the wind blows
through the trees at night
I remember how we used to
listen together
nights you slept over.

I didn't want you to move away.
You didn't want to either.
Janey
maybe some day
we'll grow up
and live near each other
again.

I wish you hadn't moved away.

Priscilla, Meet Felicity

from **Best Enemies**
by Kathleen Leverich
illustrated by Len Ebert

That September morning Priscilla woke up early.

"Hurry and dress," said her mother. "You do not want to be late for the first day of school."

Priscilla washed her face. She brushed her teeth. She put on her favorite dress. She put on her socks and her shoes. She opened her drawer, took out her brand-new pencil case, and zipped it open. Inside lay a pink eraser, a blue ballpoint pen, a red marker, and two yellow pencils with sharp points. Priscilla zipped the case shut and carried it downstairs to breakfast.

"Rrrruf," barked her dog Pow-wow.

"Don't you look nice," said her mother.

"A regular little schoolgirl," said her father.

"Big deal," said her older sister Eve. "Would somebody please pass the orange juice?"

Priscilla felt a little nervous. "What if none of my friends are in my class?"

"Wrrouu," yipped Pow-wow.

Her mother placed a bowl of cereal in front of Priscilla. She gave her a hug. "Then you will meet new friends."

Priscilla was not so sure.

Priscilla and her mother read the class lists that were posted in the school's front hall.

"There is my name!" Priscilla pointed to the fourth list. "Priscilla Robin."

"Ms. Cobble's class," read Priscilla's mother. "Room 7."

"Is Jill in my class?" asked Priscilla.

"No," said her mother.

"Is Sue in my class?" said Priscilla. "Is Dennis?"

"I am afraid not." Priscilla's mother was looking down the list, too. "Here is a nice name, 'Felicity Doll.' She sounds like a brand-new friend."

Ms. Cobble stood in the doorway to Room 7. "Good morning." She shook hands with Priscilla's mother. "Good morning." She shook hands with Priscilla. "What a lovely new pencil case!"

Ms. Cobble gave Priscilla a big name tag to hang around her neck. "Go right inside," she told Priscilla. "Choose an empty desk and sit down."

Priscilla kissed her mother goodbye. She stepped into the classroom. Lots of boys and girls chattered in the room. Priscilla felt too shy to look at them carefully. She held her pencil case tightly. She looked at the desks.

Most of the desks had a flat top and an opening at one end where you could slide books inside. A few desks looked different. They were big and old. They were made of wood and had slanted tops. The tops opened upward like the top of Priscilla's toy chest. Priscilla watched a boy put his books inside one of those desks. He lifted the desktop high.

"Wow!" thought Priscilla. "I would like one of those desks with the slanty tops." She looked around the classroom. She saw an empty desk near the blackboard. It had a flat top. She saw an empty desk near the coat closet. It had a flat top. She saw an empty desk near the front of the room. It was big and old. It was made of wood and it had a slanty top. Priscilla hurried to the desk. She pulled out a chair and sat down.

"Hey!" said a voice.

Priscilla turned. Beside her stood a curly-haired girl. She wore a ruffly dress. The name on her name tag was too difficult for Priscilla to read.

"You will have to move," said the curly-haired girl. "This desk belongs to me."

64

Priscilla felt uncertain. Then she felt mad. "This desk was empty when I sat down," she told the curly-haired girl. Priscilla opened the desk. She put her pencil case inside. Beside it she put her lunch box. "This desk is mine."

The curly-haired girl looked at the pencil case. She looked at the lunch box. She smiled a snakey smile at Priscilla. "We could share this desk. Sharing would be the fair thing to do."

"I don't want to share," said Priscilla.

The curly-haired girl poked her in the chest. "Let me share this desk, or I will tell Ms. Cobble you are being selfish."

Priscilla pushed the curly-haired girl's finger away. "All right. But just for now."

"Oh, boy!" said the girl. She dragged up a chair. She jammed it next to Priscilla's. "Move over!" Priscilla had to sit so that one leg was under the desk and one leg was outside it.

At the front of the room Ms. Cobble clapped her hands. "Let's settle down, class."

"Hey," the curly-haired girl nudged Priscilla. She pointed to Priscilla's name tag. "What does that say?"

"Priscilla," she said. She looked at the curly-haired girl's name tag. "What does yours say?"

The curly-haired girl fluffed her curls. "Don't you know how to read?" She pointed to her tag and spelled, "F-e-l-i-c-i-t-y. Felicity Doll."

Ms. Cobble handed out paper. She handed out crayons. She said, "Now, class—"

Felicity raised her hand. "Ms. Cobble!" She waved her hand as hard as she could. "Ms. Cobble!"

"Is something wrong, Felicity?" said Ms. Cobble.

Felicity squirmed in her seat. "I cannot work very well. Priscilla is crowding me."

Ms. Cobble walked over to where they sat. "What are you two girls doing at the same desk? There are plenty of empty ones. Come, Priscilla. We'll find you a desk of your own."

"But—" said Priscilla.

"Come along," said Ms. Cobble. "We have more things to do this morning than choose desks." She led Priscilla to an ordinary desk with a flat top in the very back row of the classroom. "Now," she said. "Aren't you more comfortable at a desk of your own?"

"Ms. Cobble!" Felicity waved her hand. "Priscilla left this stuff in my desk." She took out Priscilla's lunch box and pencil case and carried them back to Priscilla's new desk.

"Thank you, Felicity," said Ms. Cobble. "I can see that you are going to be an outstanding Class Helper."

Ms. Cobble returned to the front of the room. Felicity returned to her seat.

"Now, class," said Ms. Cobble.

Felicity turned around. "Hey, Priscilla!" she whispered.

"What?"

Felicity stuck out her tongue. She covered her mouth and laughed a silent laugh.

"How was your first day of school?" said Priscilla's father that night at dinner.

"Terrible," said Priscilla.

"Rrrrgrrrr." Pow-wow lay under the table at her feet.

"Did you make new friends?" asked her mother.

"I made a new enemy," said Priscilla. "Her name is Felicity Doll. She stole my desk."

"Felicity Doll?" said Eve. "I know Felicity Doll. Felicity Doll is a real snake."

"Eve!" said Priscilla's mother. She was serving the salad. "I am sure Felicity is a lovely girl, once you get to know her."

Eve shook her head. "The one thing worse than having Felicity Doll for an enemy would be having Felicity Doll for a friend."

"I do not need to worry about that," Priscilla said.

The next morning when Priscilla arrived at school she found Felicity waiting beside her desk. "This is an okay desk," said Felicity. "But my desk is much nicer."

"You stole that desk from me," said Priscilla. She sat down in her chair. She took her pencil case out of her desk. She took out a piece of paper and began to copy the new words Ms. Cobble had written on the blackboard.

Felicity stood beside Priscilla's desk. "Don't be mad, Priscilla. It is not my fault that Ms. Cobble made you move." Felicity leaned on the desk. "I like you, Priscilla."

Priscilla looked up from her paper. She could not believe her ears.

Felicity grabbed Priscilla's hand and squeezed it. "Be my friend. You can sleep over at my house. You can sit next to me at my birthday party. . . ." Felicity smiled her snakey smile.

"I have never slept over at a friend's house," said Priscilla. "My sister Eve goes on sleep-overs all the time."

"I have canopy beds," coaxed Felicity. "I have a color TV in my room. . . ."

Priscilla freed her hand from Felicity's. "Canopy beds?" Perhaps Felicity was not so bad. "Very well," she said. "I will be your friend."

"Oh, boy!" said Felicity. "Now we can swap pencil cases." She grabbed Priscilla's brand-new pencil case. She pulled her own case from her pocket and dropped it on the desk.

Felicity's case was a mess. The zipper was broken. Inside were two stubby pencils with chew marks. Nothing else.

"I do not want to swap," said Priscilla.

"Just for today." Felicity smiled her snakey smile. "Friends share."

Brnnnnggg! The bell rang.

"So long, pal," Felicity took Priscilla's pencil case and hurried to her desk.

"Felicity!" Priscilla started after her.

"Priscilla, school has begun!" clapped Ms. Cobble.
"No more visiting with Felicity. Sit down."

Priscilla sat.

"Now, class," said Ms. Cobble.

Felicity turned around at her desk. "Hey, Priscilla,"
she hissed. She waved Priscilla's pencil case and
snickered.

"How was your second day of school?" asked Priscilla's father that night at dinner.

"Terrible!" said Priscilla.

"Rrrrgrr," barked Pow-wow from under the dinner table.

"Did you make new friends?" asked Priscilla's mother.

Priscilla stuck her fork prongs into the tablecloth. "Felicity Doll wants to be my friend."

"That's nice," said Priscilla's mother. She passed Priscilla a plate of beef stew. "I am glad you two girls made up."

"Pris-cil-la," said Eve. "May I see you for a moment in the kitchen?"

Priscilla followed Eve through the swinging door.

Pow-wow followed Priscilla.

Eve shook her head. "You've been at school two days, Priscilla, and you've already made a giant mistake."

"Making friends with Felicity?" guessed Priscilla.

"Felicity does not know how to be a friend," said Eve. "Felicity knows how to be a snake."

"Rrrrgrr," barked Pow-wow.

Priscilla nodded. "Yesterday Felicity stole my desk. Today she took my pencil case."

"You need someone to stick up for you," said Eve. "Do you want me to make Felicity give your things back?"

Priscilla wanted her things back. "But," she thought, "Felicity will trap me again with another one of her tricks. . . ."

"Eve?" called their mother from the dining room. "Priscilla? Dinner is getting cold!"

"Thank you," Priscilla told Eve. "But I think I'd better stick up for myself."

The next morning Felicity wanted to trade lunch boxes.

"I have a lunch box," said Priscilla. "You carry your lunch in a paper bag."

"Friends share." Felicity smiled her snakey smile.

Before Priscilla knew what happened, Felicity carried off

Priscilla's lunch box. Felicity put the lunch box
inside the beautiful desk that should have been
Priscilla's. She put it right next to the brand-
new pencil case that Priscilla could only see
from a distance.

At lunch Felicity spilled tomato juice on her
pink sweater.

"Friends share," Felicity told Priscilla. Before
Priscilla knew it, Felicity had taken Priscilla's soft
yellow sweater.

"What will I do with this?" Priscilla wrinkled her
nose. Felicity had left her the soggy pink mess.

"Felicity Doll has gone too far!" Eve said to
Priscilla after dinner that night. "She took your
pencil case, and your lunch box, and now your
sweater—"

"Don't forget my desk," said Priscilla.

"She cannot push around my little sister!" Eve
made a fist. "Tomorrow—"

"Eve," said Priscilla, "let me try one last time."

The next morning Priscilla arrived at school.
Felicity waited beside her desk.

"I did not do my homework," said Felicity. "Lend me your paper. I will copy the answers."

Priscilla opened her mouth to say "NO!"

"Well?" said Felicity.

Priscilla shut her mouth. She had an idea. "Here is my homework." She handed Felicity her paper. She smiled a Felicity smile.

"Friends share," she said.

Felicity looked at the paper. She looked hard at Priscilla. "Is there something wrong with this homework——?"

Brnnnnggg! The bell rang.

"Settle down, class." Ms. Cobble clapped her hands.

Felicity snatched Priscilla's paper and hurried to her seat.

Priscilla watched Felicity take off *her* soft yellow sweater. She watched Felicity hang it over the back of *her* chair. She watched Felicity take a brand-new pencil out of *her* pencil case. Felicity began to copy *her* homework—

"Ms. Cobble!" Priscilla raised her hand. She waved it.

Ms. Cobble turned from the blackboard. "Priscilla, whatever is the trouble?"

Priscilla took a deep breath. "Felicity Doll is sitting at my desk."

Ms. Cobble looked at Felicity. She looked at Priscilla. "We already settled this matter, Priscilla."

"Ask Felicity whose lunch box is in that desk," said Priscilla.

"Felicity?" said Ms. Cobble.

"Wel-l-l-l," said Felicity.

"Ask her whose pencil case is in that desk," said Priscilla.

Ms. Cobble looked stern.

"Uhnnn—" said Felicity.

"That is my yellow sweater hanging over the back of Felicity's chair," said Priscilla.

Ms. Cobble frowned.

Felicity looked at her feet.

"That is my homework on top of the desk," said Priscilla.

"Fe-li-city!" said Ms. Cobble. "Is this true?"

Felicity's voice sounded squeaky. "Yes."

"Priscilla," said Ms. Cobble. "Felicity, I think you had better change desks."

"I'll get you," hissed Felicity as she passed Priscilla.

Priscilla sat down at the beautiful desk. "I doubt it," she thought.

"How was school today?" asked Priscilla's father that night at dinner.

"Rrrruf," yipped Pow-wow.

"Excellent," said Priscilla.

Priscilla's mother asked, "Did you play with your friend, Felicity Doll?"

"Felicity Doll is no longer my friend," said Priscilla. "Please pass the brussels sprouts."

"Not your friend?" Priscilla's mother looked concerned. "Whatever happened?"

Eve choked on her macaroni. "Yes, Priscilla, tell us what happened."

Pow-wow yawned. "Eeeehh."

Priscilla took a sip of milk. She smoothed the sleeves of her soft yellow sweater. "After school today, Felicity stopped me. She told me that we are no longer friends. 'We are enemies!' she said."

Priscilla's mother sighed.

Priscilla's father shook his head.

"Felicity has a new best friend," said Priscilla. "Her name is Lucille Bingay."

"How sad!" said Eve, but she was giggling. "You must feel just awful."

Priscilla speared a brussels sprout. "I don't feel nearly as awful as poor Lucille."

Priscilla, Meet Felicity

Meet the Author

Kathleen Leverich writes humorously about problems, such as jealousy and fears, that she remembers from her own childhood. Even though many of her memories are about difficult situations, she turns them into fun stories that help readers figure out how to handle their own problems.

Meet the Illustrator

Len Ebert has always wanted to be an artist, and he feels fortunate to have a career he loves. Len's career as an artist also allowed him to work at home and to be around for all of his children's activities. He says, ". . . *during all my years illustrating, there has always been a joy in doing interesting assignments . . . and working with great people! I always feel enthusiastic each time I start a new assignment . . . and always try to make it my best.*"

Theme Connections

Think About It

Now you have many stories about friendship to think about. You might want to think about these ideas:

- Felicity said she wanted a friend. How did Priscilla know that she really did not want a friend?
- Sometimes we can learn about something by looking at its opposite. Was this story about friendship or the opposite of friendship? How can you tell?

Check the Concept/Question Board to see if there are questions there that you can answer now. If the story has raised any new questions about friendship, put the questions on the Concept/Question Board. Maybe the next story will help answer the questions.

Record Ideas

 Has anything like this ever happened to you? What did you do? Priscilla trusted her feelings. How did this help her? Write your ideas about the story in your Writing Journal.

How Do Friends Behave?

Make a list of things you can do if someone is picking on you. Compare your list with your classmates'. Post a class list on the Concept/Question Board.

FINE Art

Conjunction. 1971. **Romare Bearden.** Piquette. © Romare Bearden Foundation/Licensed by VAGA, New York, NY.

Children Had Few Toys. c. 1914–17.
William Barnhill. Silver gelatin print.
Library of Congress.

***The Good
Friends.*** c. 1864.
Honoré Daumier.
Pen, brush and ink,
conte crayon,
watercolor, and
charcoal on wove
paper. 236 × 303
mm. The Baltimore
Museum of Art.
George A. Lucas
Collection. BMA
1996.48.18684.

The Tree House

Lois Lowry
illustrated by Trina Schart Hyman

It was a terrific tree house. *Better* than terrific: It was a marvelous, magnificent, one-of-a-kind tree house, with wooden walls painted bright blue. It had two windows, with red shutters on each, and a yellow door with two shiny brass hinges and a small brass bell that rang when you pulled a string. There was a little porch where you could sit with your legs dangling.

Inside were a table, a chair, a small rug with fringe on each end, and two fat pillows so that you could lie on the rug and read.

You reached it by climbing a ladder—a ladder to the best tree house ever. And it belonged to Chrissy.

"It's all mine, isn't it?" she had asked her grandfather after he built the house for her. "Just mine, and nobody else's?"

Grandpa was washing his paintbrush. He nodded. "I built it just for you," he said.

So Chrissy used her markers and made a sign. CHRISSY'S HOUSE, the sign said. KEEP OUT! She tacked it to the door. Then she took her favorite books into the tree house, curled up on the pillows, and began to read.

"Chrissy?" The voice came from the next yard, from just across the fence.

Chrissy got up and looked through the tree house window. "Hi, Leah," she said to the girl who lived next door. "How do you like my tree house, now that it's all done?"

"It's beautiful," Leah said. "What do you have inside?"

"A table and two chairs and a rug and some pillows," Chrissy told her. "And some secret stuff," she added, though she didn't have secret stuff, really. She *planned* to.

"Can I come up and see?" Leah asked.

"No," Chrissy said. "It's just for me. That's why I made the sign."

Leah stood silently for a moment. Then she said, "I hate you, Chrissy."

"I hate you, too," Chrissy replied. She went back to the pillows and opened her book again.

A short time later, she heard voices in the next yard. She peered through her window and saw that Leah's father was there with Leah. They had a wheelbarrow full of old boards, and a jar of nails. As Chrissy watched from her window, she saw Leah's father prop an old ladder against the trunk of the tree on the other side of the fence. Then, after he jiggled the ladder and made certain it was steady, he climbed up, carrying a board, and began to nail it into place where the branches came together.

He was making Leah a tree house. Chrissy laughed to herself. Leah's father was at home because he had lost his job. She knew they didn't have extra money now for things like paint and brass hinges. And Leah's tree house would never be as good as hers. Never in a million years. Chrissy went back to her book and turned the pages while the hammering continued.

That evening, after supper, Chrissy stood beside the fence and looked up at Leah's finished house. She laughed aloud.

It had taken a week for Grandpa to finish building her beautiful tree house. Grandpa had used new wooden boards from the lumberyard. But Leah's had been completed in a day, and Chrissy could see that it was made from the stack of old weathered boards that had been in the corner of Leah's yard. Only one board remained there now; the others had become the tree house.

The house had walls and a porch and a door and two windows, but it had no shutters and no paint and no door bell. The boards were crooked, and the roof had holes where the pieces of wood didn't quite meet.

Even the sign wasn't as good, because Leah had done hers with crayons instead of marking pens. But its message was the same. LEAH'S HOUSE, it said. KEEP OUT.

Leah's head appeared in the window of her tree house.

"Your house is not as nice as mine," Chrissy told her.

"Not on the outside," Leah said. "But inside, it's better."

Chrissy wondered what Leah had inside her tree house. But she didn't ask.

For several days the two girls didn't speak to each other. They sat alone in their tree houses. By the fourth day, Chrissy had finished all her books and had read some of them twice. She went to her window and called across the fence to Leah.

"Do you have any books I can borrow?" she asked, when Leah's head appeared.

"No. Our car's broken so we can't go to the library."

"You don't have any books at *all?*"

Leah shook her head.

Chrissy sat back down. She wondered what it would be like to be in a tree house with no books at all. She wondered what Leah was doing in there.

Finally she called across the fence again. "Would you like to borrow some of mine?" she asked. And Leah said yes.

So Chrissy climbed down, stood at the fence, and handed two books over to Leah, who had climbed down her ladder, too.

"I have some bananas," Leah told her. "Do you want one?" Chrissy nodded, and Leah climbed up and returned with a banana to pass across the fence.

Back in her own tree house, Chrissy peeled and ate the banana. Then she called to Leah again.

"Do you have a wastebasket in your house? I don't want to mess up my carpeting with this banana peel."

Leah, looking through her window, nodded. So Chrissy climbed down, and Leah climbed down, and Chrissy handed the banana peel across the fence.

Both girls climbed back into their houses. Chrissy sat alone and admired her fringed rug for a moment, then leafed through her books again, wondering what Leah was doing. She called through her window.

"Leah?"

Leah looked out. "What?"

"I could come visit you if you want," Chrissy said.

Leah didn't answer.

"Or you could come visit me," Chrissy added.

"Your sign says KEEP OUT," Leah pointed out. "So does mine."

"Well," Chrissy suggested, "we could change them."

Leah nodded. Each girl removed her sign and crossed out the words KEEP OUT. They wrote WELCOME instead. They rehung their signs.

"You know what, Chrissy?" Leah said. "We could use that wide board in the corner of my yard. It would go from your porch to my porch, over the top of the fence. Then we could visit each other by walking across the board."

Chrissy eyed the distance and the height. "What if we fell?"

"It's not very high," Leah pointed out. "And if we each came out halfway and held hands, we could help each other across."

They climbed down their ladders. The wide board was heavy, but when each girl took an end they were able to lift it into place. In a few minutes they had made a bridge between the houses, over the top of the fence.

Chrissy stepped from her tree house porch onto the wide board, reached for Leah's waiting hand, and walked across. She entered Leah's tree house and looked around.

There was no rug, and the only books were her own that Leah had borrowed. But there was a bowl of fruit, a wastebasket, and curtains at the windows. The walls were covered with portraits of beautiful women—the most beautiful women Chrissy had ever seen.

"I like your art collection, Leah," Chrissy said.

"They're left over from where my mom works," Leah explained. "She works at a beauty parlor, and they get pictures of all the new hairstyles. These are last year's."

"You can't tell. They look brand new."

"My house isn't as nice as yours," Leah added. "I said it was better inside, but it isn't, really."

"I don't really have carpeting," Chrissy admitted. "Only an old rug. And I don't have curtains, or a single picture on my walls."

"I could let you have one of my pictures. Two, even. You can have the blonde shag and the auburn blunt cut."

"My grandpa had paint left over. He could paint the outside of your house so we'd match. But I'm afraid we don't have another door bell."

"Now that my sign says WELCOME, I don't think I need a door bell," Leah said.

"I don't really hate you, Leah," Chrissy said.

"I don't really hate you, either," Leah replied.

They sat together on Leah's porch and looked around happily.

"What do you think is the best part of a tree house, Chrissy?" Leah asked.

Chrissy thought. She looked over at her own house, with its shutters and brass hinges. She looked around at Leah's, with its bowl of bright apples and its yellow curtains.

"The *very* best part," she said finally, "is the bridge."

The Tree House

Meet the Author

Lois Lowry was born in Honolulu, Hawaii. Her father was in the Army, so the family lived in many different places. She even attended junior high school in Tokyo, Japan. Lowry taught herself to read before she was four years old when she realized that letters made sounds, sounds made words, words made sentences, and sentences made stories. She was so excited by her discovery that she says, *"It was then that I decided that one day I would write books."* She wrote her first children's book when she was forty years old, in honor of her sister Helen who died of cancer. Since then she has published many children's stories, some of them based upon the lives of her own children.

Meet the Illustrator

Trina Schart Hyman worked many years before she became a famous children's illustrator. She started drawing when she was young and went on

to art schools in her hometown of Philadelphia, Pennsylvania. While living in Sweden, she got her first job illustrating *Pippi Longstocking*. It took her only two weeks. She later returned to the United States and had many rejections before getting work as an illustrator. In 1985 she won a Caldecott Award, one of the most important awards for children's books, for *Saint George and the Dragon*. Trina Schart Hyman is known for using people from her life, including her neighbors, friends, their children, and her children, in her illustrations.

Theme Connections

Think About It

Friends can really cause problems sometimes. Think about how people cause problems in their friendships and what they can do to fix those problems. Use the following ideas to help you begin:

- Why do friends sometimes hurt each other's feelings?
- How is this story like the other stories you have read?
- What new things have you learned about friendship?

Check the Concept/Question Board to see if there are questions there that you can answer now. If the story has raised any new questions about friendship, put the questions on the Concept/Question Board. Maybe the next story will help answer the questions.

Record Ideas

Did you ever have an argument with a friend? Did the story give you any ideas about how to make up with a friend? Write your thoughts about the story in your Writing Journal.

Building Bridges

Chrissy and Leah mended their friendship by building a bridge. Work with a partner to think of good ways to make up with a friend. Draw a bridge like the one between the tree houses. On the bridge write ways to fix a broken friendship.

How Dog Outwitted Leopard

from *Tales from the Story Hat*

an African folktale retold by Verna Aardema
illustrated by Elton Fax

In the early days in Uganda, Dog and Leopard
were friends. They lived together in a cave,
sharing the work and sharing their food.

But Leopard was stronger and bolder than Dog,
and a better hunter. Before long Dog began to grow
fat on the game brought in by his partner. The fatter
he grew, the lazier he became, until he stopped
hunting altogether.

At first Dog tried to cover up his failure to bring
home meat. He invented stories about wart hogs or
rabbits which he had *almost* caught. After a time he
decided he must think of a better way of deceiving
his friend.

And he did.

One evening Leopard said, "I've been watching a black goat down in the village of people. I think it is fat enough for eating, and tonight I'm going to get it."

"Did you say a *black* goat?" asked Dog. "That's odd. I've had my eye on a black goat, too. I think I shall go hunting myself tonight."

The two friends slept until the darkest hour just before the dawn. Then they loped off to the village. They parted near the village fence, Dog going one way and Leopard the other.

Dog ran a little way, then retraced his steps and followed Leopard from a little distance.

Leopard picked his way along the fence until he came to a goat pen. Then he backed away, gave a run, and easily cleared the palings. He killed the black goat, flung it over his shoulder, and leaped back over the fence.

At that moment Dog beat the ground and the fence with a big stick. He changed his voice and shouted, "Leopard has stolen a goat! Catch him! Catch him! There he goes! Give me that spear!"

Leopard thought the whole village was after him. He dropped the goat and ran for his life.

Then Dog trotted over, picked up the goat, and dragged it home to the cave.

"Come and see my goat!" he called to Leopard. "Isn't it a fat one! Where's your goat?"

Leopard told him of his bad luck.

"What a shame!" said Dog. "You and I will share this one."

Leopard helped build a fire to cook the goat.

When the meat was almost ready, Dog slipped out of the cave. He ran to a place just out of sight of the entrance and began beating the ground with a stick. "Ou! Ou!" he shouted. "Don't kill me! It was Leopard who killed your goat! Ou! Ou! Ou!"

Back in the cave Leopard said to himself, "The men have tracked me to my den. They are killing Dog and they will kill me next." And off he streaked into the forest.

When Dog saw that his trick had worked, he went back into the cave and ate the goat all by himself.

At dusk Leopard returned and saw Dog lying all stretched out, too full of meat to move.

Dog moaned, "Don't touch me, my friend. Those men nearly killed me! In fact they left me for dead!"

"Poor fellow!" said Leopard. "Just lie there and rest. Nothing heals like a good rest. I'll fetch us another goat soon."

Two nights later, Leopard went hunting again. Dog sneaked after him and tricked him as before, bringing in the goat himself, and then eating it himself.

Leopard was very much embarrassed by his failures. He still hadn't caught on to Dog's treachery. He decided to seek help from Muzimu, the spirit of the forest.

He found Muzimu deep in the heart of the jungle where vines coil around the trees and hang in long loops over a little black pool.

Leopard called into the pool. "Oh, Muzimu, have pity on me! Once I was a matchless hunter. Now I am dying of hunger. Though I still catch my prey, I am always driven away from it. Tell me, Muzimu, how my good luck may return."

Leopard listened. From deep down in the pool came a faint voice.

"Watch Dog. You know how to catch prey. Dog knows how to eat it. Watch Dog!"

Leopard couldn't understand how watching his friend would make his good luck return, but he decided to follow the advice.

The next night Leopard said, "I have spotted a tan goat that looks good to me. I am going to try to get it and *keep* it, this time."

"A *tan* goat?" said Dog. "I know where there are some tan goats, too. I think I'll go hunting with you tonight."

The two traveled together to the edge of the village, then separated just as before.

Leopard leaped over the fence near the goat pen, killed a tan goat, and leaped back over the palings with it.

Dog, who was hiding nearby, began threshing about, beating the fence and calling out in a strange voice. "Leopard has stolen a goat! Kill him!"

This time Leopard did not run away. He ran toward the commotion. Then he saw Dog's ears sticking up above the tall grass.

Suddenly Leopard knew who had been frightening him! With a snarl he lunged after Dog.

Round and round the village, Dog ran for his life. At last he found an opening under the fence and squeezed through just in time.

In his terror he streaked across a garden and straight into the hut of a man.

The man leaped out of bed, caught up his spear, and was about to kill Dog. But that clever creature crouched low with his head between his forepaws and his tail wagging furiously. He cocked his head and looked into Man's face. He whimpered softly, and Man understood that all he wanted was to be his friend.

And to this day, Man and Dog are fast friends, but Leopard and Dog are sworn enemies.

How Dog Outwitted Leopard

Meet the Author

Verna Aardema has always been a storyteller. When she was a girl, she used to slip away from her chores to go and tell stories to the neighborhood children. When she grew up, she became a teacher of first- and second-grade children. She had two children of her own who were often the first to hear the stories she made up. She says that being a mother helped her start writing. *". . . it was my little daughter who got me writing children's stories. She wouldn't eat without a story. And she could make a scrambled egg last all the way through 'Little Red Riding Hood.' After a time, I began to make up little feeding stories. Because I was usually reading about Africa, the feeding stories were apt to be set in Ashantiland or the Kalahari Desert."*

Meet the Illustrator

Elton Fax often borrowed books from the public library as a child. He particularly enjoyed the classic fairy tales with their beautiful illustrations. But his special favorite was a series of travel books for children called *Our Little Cousins*. He says, *"How I enjoyed reading about our little cousins from far off and often exotic lands—Armenia, Bolivia, Latvia, Georgia, Kenya, Argentina, Uruguay, Italy, Uganda, Ethiopia, Nigeria. . . . How little indeed did I ever dream I would not only visit such places but that I would be making drawings in them and later writing about them so that others could share what I have seen and heard and felt."*

Theme Connections

Think About It

How can you tell the difference between real friends and false friends? Here are some ideas to think about:

- Why did it take so long for Leopard to find out about Dog's tricks?
- What does trust have to do with friendship?
- How is this story like "Priscilla, Meet Felicity"?

Check the Concept/Question Board to see if there are questions there that you can answer now. If the story has raised any new questions about friendship, put the questions on the Concept/Question Board. Maybe the next story will help answer the questions.

Record Ideas

Has someone tricked you? What did you do? What did you learn? Write about it in your Writing Journal. How do you think writers turn their memories into stories?

All About Friendship

You have read about good friends and false friends. Look at the posters you have done as a class. What new things have you learned about friendship? As a class, make any changes you think should be made to the posters.

Peter Golenbock
illustrated by Paul Bacon

Jackie Robinson   Pee Wee Reese

Jackie Robinson was more than just my teammate.
He had a tremendous amount of talent, ability, and dedication.
Jackie set a standard for future generations of ball players.
He was a winner. Jackie Robinson was also a man.

—PEE WEE REESE
October 31, 1989

Once upon a time in America, when automobiles were black and looked like tanks and laundry was white and hung on clotheslines to dry, there were two wonderful baseball leagues that no longer exist. They were called the Negro Leagues.

The Negro Leagues had extraordinary players, and adoring fans came to see them wherever they played. They were heroes, but players in the Negro Leagues didn't make much money and their lives on the road were hard.

Laws against segregation didn't exist in the 1940s. In many places in this country, black people were not allowed to go to the same schools and churches as white people. They couldn't sit in the front of a bus or trolley car. They couldn't drink from the same drinking fountains that white people drank from.

Satchel Paige

Back then, many hotels didn't rent rooms to black people, so the Negro League players slept in their cars. Many towns had no restaurants that would serve them, so they often had to eat meals that they could buy and carry with them.

Life was very different for the players in the Major Leagues. They were the leagues for white players. Compared to the Negro League players, white players were very well paid. They stayed in good hotels and ate in fine restaurants. Their pictures were put on baseball cards and the best players became famous all over the world.

Branch Rickey

Many Americans knew that racial prejudice was wrong, but few dared to challenge openly the way things were. And many people were apathetic about racial problems. Some feared that it could be dangerous to object. Vigilante groups, like the Ku Klux Klan, reacted violently against those who tried to change the way blacks were treated.

The general manager of the Brooklyn Dodgers baseball team was a man by the name of Branch Rickey. He was not afraid of change. He wanted to treat the Dodger fans to the best players he could find, regardless of the color of their skin. He thought segregation was unfair and wanted to give everyone, regardless of race or creed, an opportunity to compete equally on ballfields across America.

To do this, the Dodgers needed one special man.

Branch Rickey launched a search for him. He was looking for a star player in the Negro Leagues who would be able to compete successfully despite threats on his life or attempts to injure him. He would have to possess the self-control not to fight back when opposing players tried to intimidate or hurt him. If this man disgraced himself on the field, Rickey knew, his opponents would use it as an excuse to keep blacks out of Major League baseball for many more years.

Rickey thought Jackie Robinson might be just the man.

Jackie rode the train to Brooklyn to meet Mr. Rickey. When Mr. Rickey told him, "I want a man with the courage not to fight back," Jackie Robinson replied, "If you take this gamble, I will do my best to perform." They shook hands. Branch Rickey and Jackie Robinson were starting on what would be known in history as "the great experiment."

Branch Rickey and Jackie Robinson.

At spring training with the Dodgers, Jackie was mobbed by blacks, young and old, as if he were a savior. He was the first black player to try out for a Major League team. If he succeeded, they knew, others would follow.

Initially, life with the Dodgers was for Jackie a series of humiliations. The players on his team who came from the South, men who had been taught to avoid black people since childhood, moved to another table whenever he sat down next to them. Many opposing players were cruel to him, calling him nasty names from their dugouts. A few tried to hurt him with their spiked shoes. Pitchers aimed at his head. And he received threats on his life, both from individuals and from organizations like the Ku Klux Klan.

Team photo of the 1947 Brooklyn Dodgers.

Despite all the difficulties, Jackie Robinson didn't give up. He made the Brooklyn Dodgers team.

But making the Dodgers was only the beginning. Jackie had to face abuse and hostility throughout the season, from April through September. His worst pain was inside. Often he felt very alone. On the road he had to live by himself, because only the white players were allowed in the hotels in towns where the team played.

The whole time Pee Wee Reese, the Dodger shortstop, was growing up in Louisville, Kentucky, he had rarely even seen a black person, unless it was in the back of a bus. Most of his friends and relatives hated the idea of his playing on the same field as a black man. In addition, Pee Wee Reese had more to lose than the other players when Jackie joined the team.

Jackie Robinson.

Jackie had been a shortstop, and everyone thought that Jackie would take Pee Wee's job. Lesser men might have felt anger toward Jackie, but Pee Wee was different. He told himself, "If he's good enough to take my job, he deserves it."

When his Southern teammates circulated a petition to throw Jackie off the team and asked him to sign it, Pee Wee responded, "I don't care if this man is black, blue or striped"—and refused to sign. "He can play and he can help us win," he told the others. "That's what counts."

Very early in the season, the Dodgers traveled west to Ohio to play the Cincinnati Reds. Cincinnati is near Pee Wee's hometown of Louisville.

The Reds played in a small ballpark where the fans sat close to the field. The players could almost feel the breath of the fans on the backs of their necks. Many who came that day screamed terrible, hateful things at Jackie when the Dodgers were on the field.

More than anything else, Pee Wee Reese believed in doing what was right. When he heard the fans yelling at Jackie, Pee Wee decided to take a stand.

With his head high, Pee Wee walked directly from his shortstop position to where Jackie was playing first base. The taunts and shouting of the fans were ringing in Pee Wee's ears. It saddened him, because he knew it could have been his friends and neighbors. Pee Wee's legs felt heavy, but he knew what he had to do.

As he walked toward Jackie wearing the gray Dodger uniform, he looked into his teammate's bold, pained eyes. The first baseman had done nothing to provoke the hostility except that he sought to be treated as an equal. Jackie was grim with anger. Pee Wee smiled broadly as he reached Jackie. Jackie smiled back.

Stopping beside Jackie, Pee Wee put his arm around Jackie's shoulders. An audible gasp rose up from the crowd when they saw what Pee Wee had done. Then there was silence.

Outlined on a sea of green grass stood these two great athletes, one black, one white, both wearing the same team uniform.

"I am standing by him," Pee Wee Reese said to the world. "This man is my teammate."

Meet the Author

Peter Golenbock is a sportswriter who especially loves baseball. He remembers going to the World Series in 1956 with his uncle and afterward meeting Jackie Robinson. He says, *"I was 12 years old, and I'll never forget being struck by how large he was."* Throughout his career Peter Golenbock has had the opportunity to meet many famous players and to hear the stories they tell about the game's history. He has even written biographies about some of the players he has talked to. He is the author of many well-known books about sports, but this book was the first one he wrote for children.

Meet the Illustrator

Paul Bacon is an award-winning illustrator and famous designer of book jackets. He lives in Clintondale, New York, with his wife.

Theme Connections

Think About It

Sometimes people become friends even when they don't expect to or want to. What surprising things are there about friendship? Use the following ideas to help you:

- Do teammates have to be friends?
- Why is it sometimes important to have a friend who will stand up for you?
- How is this story like "Gloria Who Might Be My Best Friend?"

Check the Concept/Question Board to see if there are questions there that you can answer now. If the story has raised any new questions about friendship, put the questions on the Concept/Question Board. Maybe the next story will help answer the questions.

Record Ideas

Have you made any unexpected friends on sports teams or in school clubs? Write about your experiences in your Writing Journal.

All About Friendship

Write these words on a piece of paper: "A friend is". Work with a partner to write as many words or phrases as you can think of to finish the sentence. Then share with your classmates all the ideas about friendship you have learned from reading the stories in this unit.

Bibliography

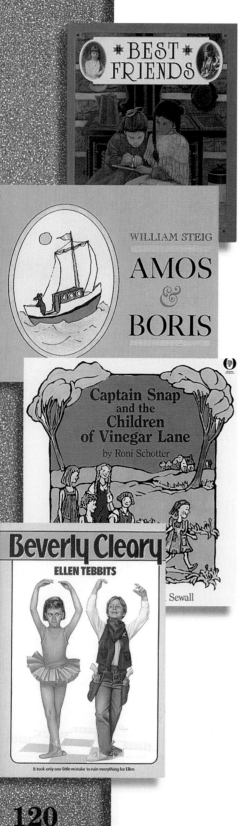

Best Friends

by Loretta Krupinski. How powerful is friendship? In this story, it is strong enough to gain freedom for a Nez Perce girl and her tribe.

Amos & Boris

by William Steig. What do a mouse and a whale have in common? Not much! But they become the best of friends and do what good friends should.

Captain Snap and the Children of Vinegar Lane

by Roni Schotter. The children of Vinegar Lane befriend crabby old Captain Snap when he is ill. What secret does their act of friendship help to uncover?

Ellen Tebbits

by Beverly Cleary. Ellen Tebbits gains a best friend when she discovers she shares the same secret with Austine Allen, the new girl in school.

Officer Buckle and Gloria

by Peggy Rathmann. For Officer Buckle and Gloria, "always stick by your buddy!" proves to be good advice for safety as well as friendship.

On Call Back Mountain

by Eve Bunting. How does a lone wolf with great shining eyes help two boys deal with the death of a friend?

Rugby and Rosie

by Nan Parson Rossiter. Read about three friends, two dogs and a boy, who have only one year together and the important reason why.

Wilfrid Gordon McDonald Partridge

by Mem Fox. A small boy asks "What's a memory?" in hopes of helping a special friend find hers.

City Wildlife

Even if you live in the city, wild things surround you. What are they? Where are they? How do they live? Maybe if you look, you will find them.

123

City Critters:

Wild Animals Live in Cities, Too

by Richard Chevat

The city. Tall buildings. Shoppers with their arms full of packages. People hurrying along. Buses, cabs, cars—and wild animals.

Wild animals? You bet. Cities and towns are filled with wildlife.

"When most people think of wildlife, they think of grizzly bears or elk or white-tailed deer. But *all* the wild animals that live in a city are wildlife, including butterflies, ants, pigeons and even rats," says Mike Matthews. He's a scientist

These city ducks might cause a traffic jam.

who works for New York state, trying to protect its wildlife, both in the woods and in the cities.

Why does a rat deserve to be called "wildlife"? Charles Nilon, a biologist for the Kansas Department of Wildlife and Parks explains: "Any animal that you see that is not a pet, that doesn't depend on people taking care of it, is a wild animal."

Skyscraper Geese, Park Raccoons

On the tenth floor of an office building in St. Louis, Missouri, is a nest of Canadian geese. They've been spending summers there for the past six years.

Dave Tylka is an urban biologist—a scientist who studies wildlife in cities. He talked about the skyscraper geese. "There's a type of Canadian geese that nest on cliffs over the Mississippi River," he said. "These particular geese must have thought that a balcony looked like a good cliff to nest on!"

If geese on an office building sound strange, how about raccoons in the heart of New York City? Mike Matthews says they live in sewers, in buildings, and especially in New York's Central Park. "People think that animals want to be near trees or open spaces. But raccoons will live in chimneys and sewers."

Raccoons live in sewers and parks. They find food in garbage cans.

Bird's-Eye View

According to Matthews, city parks are great places to go bird-watching, especially in the early spring and fall. "They're like islands of green space where migrating birds will stop," he says.

When Mike Matthews talks about birds, he doesn't just mean "city birds" like sparrows, starlings and pigeons. "There's much, much more," he says. "In the city limits, there are great blue herons, owls and all sorts of water birds. Even a bald eagle will visit from time to time."

You might think these creatures would try to avoid cities. Not so, says Matthews. Animals will live wherever they can find food, shelter and a place to raise their young.

Scientists' Helpers

Scientists can learn a lot about a city by studying the wild animals that live there. "If you're concerned about pollution or waste, looking at wildlife is one way to learn about it," says Charles Nilon, the Kansas biologist.

"For example, in Florida, scientists studied squirrels that lived by highways. The scientists wanted to find out how the squirrels had been affected by breathing car exhaust. Because they breathe the fumes all day, any health

A street light makes a good perch for this eagle.

126

Squirrels and chipmunks are common wildlife in cities.
This chipmunk is stealing some birdseed from a window ledge.

problems will show up in squirrels before they show up in humans."

Sometimes, very rare animals can survive well in cities. Take the peregrine falcon. This bird had almost disappeared in the eastern United States. About 15 years ago, scientists began trying to save the peregrine falcon by raising baby falcons in laboratories and releasing them in the wild.

Today, the bird is making a comeback, and several falcons have come back to nest in the middle of big cities. There, they've found just the right kinds of shelter and food. They rest on skyscraper "cliffs," and they hunt city birds—pigeons and starlings.

Home Sweet City Home

Not all animals find city homes as easily as falcons have. That's why scientists create and protect special animal habitats—spots with the right amounts of water and food and the kinds of trees and plants an animal needs to survive.

At the Gateway National Recreation Area in New York City, scientists have set aside a small "grasslands" habitat—a flat, open field. Don Reipe, a scientist at Gateway, explained why: "Grasslands are vanishing because they're used for homes, shopping malls and other developments. But it's an important habitat for animals like the upland sandpiper, the meadowlark and the short-eared owl. Our grasslands area is a home to all these birds."

Scientists in Des Moines, Iowa, built a different kind of habitat—a garden that grows goodies for butterflies. It's in the state fairgrounds. "We planted a garden designed to attract 40 different species of butterflies," says Laura Jackson, an Iowa biologist. "The idea is to show people how they can attract butterflies to their backyards by planting the right flowers and plants."

Deer are moving closer to cities. Some have been spotted in city parks.

Do It Yourself

Most people don't see the wild animals all around them—because they don't know what to look for. Stephen Petland, a biologist in Seattle, Washington, says careful observation—and a look at a few bird and animal guides—can make the difference.

"In one neighborhood in Seattle, over the course of a year, I might be able to find 40 or 50 different types of birds," notes Petland.

You don't have to be a scientist to study wildlife in cities or towns. Just keep an eagle eye when you're playing in your yard, your playground or your neighborhood park. And when you're walking down the street, don't forget: Watch out for wild animals!

City Critters:

Wild Animals Live in Cities, Too

Meet the Author

Richard Chevat loved to read and make up stories of his own as a child in New York City. Today he lives in New Jersey with his wife, two children, and a pet bird named Madonna. He writes at home while his children are at school and his wife is at work. *"I play the guitar, I like to cook, and spend a lot of time with my kids,"* says Mr. Chevat.

130

Theme Connections

Think About It

The theme for this unit is City Wildlife. Do you live in a city or near a city? Think about wild animals that you have seen in the city. Here are some things to think about to help you begin:

- Have you noticed any animals in places around your home or in a city you have been to? Have you really looked for them?
- What types of animals are you interested in? What do you want to learn more about?

Check the Concept/Question Board to see if there are questions there that you can answer now. If the selection has raised any new questions about city wildlife, put the questions on the Concept/Questions Board. Maybe the next selection will help answer the questions.

Record Ideas

Did the selection tell you anything you didn't already know about city wildlife? Write down how you feel about learning new things.

Write a Paragraph

Pick one type of wild animal you have noticed around your house and write a paragraph that tells what you have noticed about this animal. Share your paragraph with your classmates. Do they know something about this animal that you don't?

City Lots: Living Things in Vacant Spots

Phyllis S. Busch
illustrated by Pamela Carroll

Cities are full of buildings—all kinds of buildings. There are big homes and small ones, where people live. There are factories and offices where people work. There are schools, libraries, museums, where people learn.

Cities are also full of people. There are homemakers, housepainters, streetcleaners, shopkeepers, factory workers, firefighters, carpenters, clerks, bankers, bakers, and all their children.

But among this mass of people and their dwellings you can find some vacant spots—large or small places where there are neither people nor buildings. These are known as city lots.

Is there a city lot near where you live? Perhaps you use it as a short cut to a friend's house, or to a store, or to a bus stop.

Some city lots are just narrow shaded passageways between two buildings. Others are bright and sunny. You can find these lots on street corners, or where there are large spaces between buildings.

Was the lot in your neighborhood always vacant? Or was there once a building which was torn down? You might search for evidence such as bricks or pieces of plaster. But first make sure that the lot is a safe place to play this game of exploration.

A vacant lot is really not vacant at all. It is a place where many plants and animals live all year round. A vacant lot contains all the things plants and animals need in order to live: soil, water, air, sunlight, food, space. Here you can watch the changes that take place in living things all through the year.

In the corner
of an old city lot
you may find a London plane tree, also known as a
sycamore. This tree has surprises for every season.
In the bright spring sunshine, the brown and tan
trunk is a sparkling patchwork of colors. The bark
peelings which cause this colorful pattern lie
scattered on the ground.

Examine these before and after a rain. You will
discover that the tight bark rolls are brittle in dry
weather, and loose and softened when it is wet.
In the summer it is pleasant to sit in the shade of
a sycamore tree, under its spreading dark green
leaves. Take the temperature of the air under the
tree. How is it different from the temperature
of the air in the sunlight?

With the coming of autumn the sycamore
leaves turn brown and fall to the ground to
form a crunchy carpet. Remove a leaf not
yet fallen and find the little hollow at the
end of the leaf stalk. Notice how this forms
a cap over a new bud——a little bundle of
energy ready to start next year's growth.

Winter is the time to see the sycamore balls hanging high in the tree. A strong wind dashes them to the ground, where you can collect some and observe their seeds. How many seeds does one of these balls of fruit contain? How many trees might develop from all the seeds of one parent tree? It is a wonder that the lot is not full of sycamores.

You can also follow the seasons with the ailanthus tree, the commonest city tree. In China, where it came from, it is known as the Tree-of-Heaven. Observe it after the leaves have fallen as it stands with its stout bare branches outstretched against the sky. Large heartshaped scars show where the leaves were attached. You might see bunches of fruit up in the tree, and hear them rattle in the breeze.

Ailanthus trees grow rapidly in the spring and can occupy a large portion of a city lot. If you play in a "jungle" in your lot in summer, it is probably a tangle of these trees.

A patch of spring sunshine in the corner of a lot may gleam with the gold of dandelions.

A shadier spot might be adorned with a little violet, a spot of purple beauty even among discarded garbage and its hovering flies. Wouldn't the violet be prettier without garbage that brings flies and rats?

You learn to avoid the tangles of prickly blackberry as you explore, but you should stop to admire the rich red color of the leaves in the fall. The fruits are quickly eaten by birds.

It is often from the fall fruits left uneaten by mice and birds that new plants arise in the spring. You yourself may have helped to scatter the seeds of burdock, also known as stickers.

Run your finger up the stalk of the common plantain when it is wet. Feel the sticky seeds. All who walk over the flat-leaved plantains carry with them some seeds which are later dropped to grow into next year's crop.

It is fun to spend a year watching any one plant, and milkweed is a happy choice. Milkweed pods are beautiful whether they are open or closed. Look inside a bright green pod in early autumn. See how the many brown seeds with their silvery parachutes fit neatly into a package.

Later in the season all the fruit pods, now in shades of tan, are open. Watch the seeds float in the air on a windy day. Which way do the beautiful wisps travel? How far do they go? Will they give rise to more milkweed plants next spring? What insects will be attracted to their fragrant lavender flowers in summer?

In autumn a city lot is bound to have some tall flourishing ragweed. Although the flowers are tiny, hayfever sufferers know when the plant is in bloom. Large amounts of pollen float in the air and disturb sensitive noses. Shake some flowers over a piece of glass which is covered with a thin layer of petroleum jelly. You can then observe this flower dust under a microscope. The flowers look like miniature sculptures.

Where ragweed grows you might find a corner made bright with purple asters and yellow goldenrod.

If city lots have plants they certainly must have animals. Some insects lay their eggs in the stems of goldenrod. This causes the plant to form a swelling known as a gall. Here the young develop,

to hatch out the following spring. If you cut open a gall, you may find an immature insect.

Is there a wild black cherry tree on the lot? In the spring you might find a mass of tent caterpillars resting in a silken shelter which they have spun between supporting branches. These insects appear to have regular periods for feeding and for spinning. Observe a colony of tent caterpillars over the weeks in order to learn their routine.

Those caterpillars which are not gobbled up by hungry birds or destroyed by parasites change into brown moths. Look for their shiny dark brown bands of eggs on bare winter twigs.

Small green plant lice or aphids are frequently found feeding on the juices of stems or leaves. A praying mantis might stalk nearby, gobbling up these and other insects. The praying mantis is a large green and brown insect whose bent front legs make it appear as if it is praying. You can locate its hard brown egg mass among the winter shrubs. Over three hundred babies may hatch from one such egg case in the spring.

A city lot is a suitable habitat for many birds. They need a safe place to build a nest, as well as an adequate food supply and a source of water. Most common is the English sparrow. Observe it as it hops, flies, builds a nest, sits on its eggs, feeds spiders and flies to its young, bathes in rain pools and dusts in sandy spots.

Try to follow the habits of the pigeons which are sure to be there. Maybe there is also a robin, attracted to the cherries in the cherry tree. Are there some squawking starlings? They lead busy lives too.

Did you ever visit the lot during or after a light rainfall in spring or summer? It smells different from the rest of the city—cool and refreshing. How much cooler the air is over the lot than over the pavement. Feel the gentle raindrops on your face. Open your mouth and taste some fresh rainwater. Watch the rain strike the leaves, run down the stalks and onto the stems from where it slowly continues down into the soil. Here is where it is available to the plant roots which absorb it. Miniature streams and lakes form where there are depressions in the ground. Perhaps a puppy or a bird comes for a drink or a bath, leaving its footprints in the mud nearby.

People need places to live, to work, and to shop. But people also need open spaces. Every neighborhood should have a lot which is left without buildings—a place to rest and to play and to make new discoveries about its plants and animals.

DRINK

141

City Lots: Living Things in Vacant Spots

Meet the Author

Phyllis S. Busch has taught students in elementary and high school as well as college. She teaches about biology and the environment. For many years she has been working on projects to teach elementary students and their parents about the environment through outdoor explorations and experiments. She is involved with nearly twenty different environmental groups and has received many awards for her work in science education. She has written dozens of educational books and guides that bring science to life for children.

Meet the Illustrator

Pamela Carroll is a well-known illustrator of children's books. *The Dolphins and Me*, *Nature's Living Lights*, and *Life in a Tidal Pool* are some of the books she has illustrated. Look for some of her illustrations with other selections in the **Open Court Reading** series.

142

Theme Connections

Think About It

Have you ever thought of plants and insects as wildlife? Here are some things to help you:

- How are the plants that grow wild the same as plants that people grow? How are they different?
- Do the plants, animals, and insects help each other survive? What are some of the ways they do this?

Check the Concept/Question Board to see if there are questions there that you can answer now. If the story has raised any new questions about wildlife in the city, put the questions on the Concept/Question Board. Maybe the next story will help answer the questions.

Record Ideas

 What plants do you have around your house? Did someone plant them or did they just start growing on their own? Did this selection change any ideas you had about plants and insects? In what way? Write about the plants and insects around your house and what they mean to you.

School Grounds

The next time you leave the school building, notice the kinds of plants you see around the school. Did someone plant them? Did they grow on their own? What are some ways you can learn more about them?

The Boy Who Didn't Believe in Spring

Lucille Clifton

illustrated by Brinton Turkle

Once upon a time there was a little boy named King Shabazz who didn't believe in Spring. "No such thing!" he would whisper every time the teacher talked about Spring in school.

"Where is it at?" he would holler every time his Mama talked about Spring at home.

144

He used to sit with his friend Tony Polito on the bottom step when the days started getting longer and warmer and talk about it.

"Everybody talkin bout Spring!" he would say to Tony.

"Big deal," Tony would say back.

"No such thing!" he would say to Tony.

"Right!" Tony would say back.

One day after the teacher had been talking about birds that were blue and his Mama had started talking about crops coming up, King Shabazz decided he had just had enough. He put his jacket on and his shades and went by for Tony Polito.

"Look here, man," King said when they got out to the bottom step, "I'm goin to get me some of this Spring."

"What you mean, man?" Tony asked him.

"Everybody talkin bout Spring comin, and Spring just round the corner. I'm goin to go round there and see what do I see."

Tony Polito watched King Shabazz get up and push his shades up tight on his nose.

"You comin with me, man?" he said while he was pushing.

Tony Polito thought about it for a minute. Then he got up and turned his cap around backwards.

"Right!" Tony Polito said back.

King Shabazz and Tony Polito had been around the corner before, but only as far as the streetlight alone. They passed the school and the playground.

"Ain't no Spring in there," said King Shabazz with a laugh. "Sure ain't," agreed Tony Polito.

They passed Weissman's. They stopped for a minute by the side door at Weissman's and smelled the buns.

"Sure do smell good," whispered Tony.

"But it ain't Spring," King was quick to answer.

They passed the apartments and walked fast in case
they met Junior Williams. He had said in school that he
was going to beat them both up.

Then they were at the streetlight. Tony stopped and
made believe his sneaker was untied to see what King
was going to do. King stopped and blew on his shades
to clean them and to see what Tony was going to do.
They stood there for two light turns and then King
Shabazz grinned at Tony Polito, and he grinned back,
and the two boys ran across the street.

"Well, if we find it, it ought to be now," said King.

Tony didn't say anything. He just stood looking
around.

"Well, come on, man," King whispered, and they
started down the street.

They passed the Church of the Solid Rock with high windows all decorated and pretty.

They passed a restaurant with little round tables near the window. They came to a take-out shop and stood by the door a minute to smell the bar-b-q.

"Sure would like to have some of that," whispered King.

"Me too," whispered Tony with his eyes closed. They walked slower down the street.

Just after they passed some apartments King Shabazz and Tony Polito came to a vacant lot. It was small and had high walls from apartments on three sides of it. Three walls around it and right in the middle——a car!

It was beautiful. The wheels were gone and so were the doors, but it was dark red and sitting high on a dirt mound in the middle of the lot.

"Oh man, oh man," whispered King.

"Oh man," whispered Tony.

Then they heard the noise.

It was a little long sound, like smooth things rubbing against rough, and it was coming from the car. It happened again. King looked at Tony and grabbed his hand.

"Let's see what it is, man," he whispered. He thought Tony would say no and let's go home. Tony looked at King and held his hand tightly.

"Right," he said very slowly.

The boys stood there a minute, then began tiptoeing over toward the car. They walked very slowly across the lot. When they were halfway to the car, Tony tripped and almost fell. He looked down and saw a patch of little yellow pointy flowers, growing in the middle of short spiky green leaves.

"Man, I think you tripped on these crops!" King laughed.

"They're comin up," Tony shouted. "Man, the crops are comin up!"

And just as Tony was making all that noise, they
heard another noise, like a lot of things waving in the
air, and they looked over at the car and three birds flew
out of one of the door holes and up to the wall of the
apartment.

King and Tony ran over to the car to see where the
birds had been. They had to climb up a little to get to
the door and look in.

They stood there looking a long time without saying
anything. There on the front seat down in a whole lot
of cottony stuff was a nest. There in the nest were four
light blue eggs. Blue. King took off his shades.

"Man, it's Spring," he said almost to himself.

"Anthony Polito!"

King and Tony jumped down off the mound.
Somebody was shouting for Tony as loud as he could.

"Anthony Polito!"

The boys turned and started walking out of the
vacant lot. Tony's brother Sam was standing at the edge
of the lot looking mad.

"Ma's gonna kill you, after I get finished, you squirt!"
he hollered.

King Shabazz looked at Tony Polito and took his hand.

"Spring is here," he whispered to Tony.

"Right," whispered Tony Polito back.

The Boy Who Didn't Believe in Spring

Meet the Author

Lucille Clifton is a famous poet and writer of children's books. When she was just sixteen years old, she became the first member of her family to earn a scholarship and attend college. She knew while attending college that what she wanted most to be was a writer. However, it took her many years to reach her goal. Lucille Clifton first finished college, married, and had six children. When she did publish her first book, a book of poems called *Good Times*, the *New York Times* named it one of the ten best books of the year. Since then, she has won many awards and has become one of the most famous poets and children's authors.

Meet the Illustrator

Brinton Turkle is a famous illustrator of children's books as well as an author. He first studied drama for a while in college. Then he decided to focus more on drawing and went to school for fine arts.

He has written many famous children's books in the hope that they will teach children kindness, honesty, and a love for life.

154

Theme Connections

Think About It

This story is different from the first two. It is a fiction story. Although it still tells you something about wildlife in the city, in a story like this, you can learn information from what the characters say and how they act. Here are some things to think about:

- What kinds of homes did the wild things in this story make? Have you ever seen animals do this?
- Why are some animals called wild and others not? Why are some plants called wild and others not?

Check the Concept/Question Board to see if there are questions there that you can answer now. If the story has raised any new questions about wildlife that lives in the city, put the questions on the Concept/Question Board. Maybe the next story will help answer the questions.

Record Ideas

What is spring like where you live? Is it anything like what King and Tony found in this story? Write how you feel about the story and about spring in your Writing Journal.

Make a Chart

Work together with your classmates to make a wildlife chart. In one column, list the wildlife you have learned about. In the next column, put a check by the plants and animals that also live in your neighborhood. Add selections and information to the chart as you continue reading the selections in the unit.

FINE Art

Lunch in the Gardens. 1985. **Beryl Cook.** Oil on masonite.
From Beryl Cook's New York, John Murray Publishing.
©1998 Beryl Cook. Reproduced by arrangement with
Rogers, Coleridge & White Ltd. Photo: Flannagan
Graphics, New Jersey.

Cable Car Festival. 1988. **Dong Kingman.** Watercolor on paper. 30" × 22". Conacher Gallery, San Francisco.

Urban Roosts
Where Birds Nest in the City

from the book by
Barbara Bash

Early in the morning you can hear something rustling up on the ledge of an old stone building. Even before the city awakens, the birds are stirring in their urban roosts.

All across the country, as their natural habitats have been destroyed, birds have moved to town. The ones that have been able to adapt are thriving in the heart of the city.

One familiar urban dweller is the pigeon. Long ago it was called a rock dove, because it lived in the rocky cliffs along the coast of Europe. Today it flourishes all over the United States in the nooks and crannies of our cities.

To the pigeon, the city may look like a wilderness full of high cliffs and deep canyons. The cliffs are buildings made of stone and brick and glass, and the canyons are windy avenues full of cars and people. Flying together in flocks, pigeons explore the city canyons looking for food and spots to roost.

A roost is a place where birds go for protection when they sleep and for shelter from the rain and cold. Pigeons roost under highway overpasses, on window ledges, under building archways, on top of roofs, and under eaves. Sometimes their roosts are so well hidden you have to watch carefully to find them.

Look up under the train trestle. Pigeons may be roosting along the dark beams. Watch the open windows of an abandoned building. Hundreds of pigeons could be living inside, flying in and out all day long.

A nest is a place where birds lay their eggs and raise their chicks. Often it's in the same spot as the roost. Pigeons build a flimsy platform of sticks and twigs and debris up on a ledge, or on a windowsill, or in a flowerpot out on a fire escape, or in the curve of a storefront letter.

Throughout the year, pigeons lay eggs and hatch their young. The female sits quietly on her clutch, and after eighteen days, fuzzy chicks begin to appear. Five weeks later, after their adult feathers are fully developed, the young pigeons fly away to find homes of their own.

160

Sparrows and finches are successful city dwellers, too. Introduced from England in 1870 to control insects, the house sparrow has chosen to live close to people all across the United States. The house finch was originally a West Coast native, but some caged birds were released on the East Coast in 1940, and the species quickly spread. Sparrows and finches don't migrate, so you can watch them at backyard feeders throughout the year, chirping and chattering as they pick up seeds.

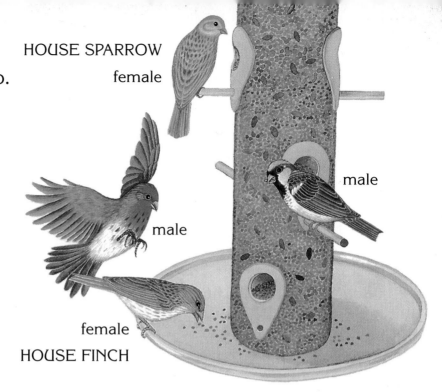

HOUSE SPARROW
female
male
male
female
HOUSE FINCH

The little hollows in and around building ornaments and Gothic sculptures are favorite nesting spots for sparrows and finches. These cavity nesters can slip into the tiniest spaces. Some of their nests are visible and others are completely hidden from view.

In the spring, you may see a small bird flying overhead with a twig in its beak. If you follow its flight, it will lead you to its nest.

161

Watch the bird land and then disappear into a crevice or behind a stone curve. A few moments later it will pop out again, empty-beaked, and fly away to search for more nesting material.

Sparrows and finches can even find spots to nest out in the middle of the busiest intersections. At the top of some streetlights, there's a small opening where the lamp meets the pole. If you look carefully, you may see a tiny house finch slip inside.

Or watch the short open pipe at the top of some traffic light poles. A pair of house sparrows may be darting in and out, bringing food to their nestlings. Sometimes you can even spot a nest in the metal casing that surrounds a traffic light. Perhaps the heat of the bulb keeps the eggs warm.

A tiled roof can house so many sparrows and finches it looks a little like an apartment complex. All day long the birds bring nesting material and food for their chicks into the small hidden cavities behind the tiles. When the chicks get too big for the nest, they play on top of the tiles, testing their wings before their first flight.

Because the house wren eats only insects, it prefers to live in the suburbs, where there are more bugs. The wren's family name is *Troglodytidae*, which means "creeper into holes." True to its name, the house wren can be found in the most unusual cavities: a work glove hanging on a line, a ball of twine, a teapot, an old shoe. Once the female wren chooses the cavity, she bolsters it with lots of nesting material to protect her eggs from intruders.

Along with the usual grasses, twigs, and feathers, wrens' nests have been found to contain hairpins, Kleenex, nails, wire, shoe buckles, candy wrappers, Band-Aids, paper clips, even dollar bills!

The barn owl lives in the city, too, but few people see it because it flies while everyone sleeps. All night long its pale, ghostly form soars over the buildings as it hunts for rats and mice to bring to its young.

The barn owl's eyes can see in the dark and its ears can hear the tiniest scratching. Even its voice is suited to city life; when it cries out in the night, it sounds like brakes screeching.

At daybreak, barn owls return to their nests to sleep. They like to live under train and highway overpasses and inside old barns and steeples. Instead of building nests, they lay their eggs in flat, protected spots. As baby barn owls grow, they huddle together, hissing and slurping, as they wait for their parents to return with food.

The nighthawk is a ground-nesting bird; it looks for a level, open surface on which to lay its eggs. Because city ground is full of cars and people, the nighthawk often hatches its young up on flat graveled rooftops.

If you look up on a warm summer night, you might see a nighthawk swooping low over the streetlights sweeping hundreds of insects into its large, gaping mouth. Or you might hear its call in the dark . . . *peent* . . . *peent* . . . .

Like the nighthawk, the killdeer makes no
nest. It lays its eggs out in the open, in
spots where the mottled eggshell pattern
will be well camouflaged. In the city you
might find killdeer eggs sitting on the gravel
at the edge of a parking lot or next to a
train track. Once, killdeer eggs were even
found along the end line of a soccer field!

During the winter, crows flock together
in large groups. They roost at night in the

tops of trees in city parks. At dusk, one or two arrive first, perching on high branches and making a silky rustle with their wings. As the light fades, more crows appear and the clamor increases. They make rattling sounds, catlike cries, and metallic squeaks while they jostle for spots. As the darkness deepens, the calls gradually die down, until only an occasional gurgle is heard. Then the crows settle in for the night.

In November, snowy owls migrate down from the arctic tundra to spend the winter in northern cities. They seem to like the windswept environment of airport landing fields—perhaps because it reminds them of home. The owls roost out on the open ground, blending in with the snowy whiteness.

At dusk the snowy owls begin hunting for mice, rats, and rabbits. They fly slowly and silently, their heads turning from side to side, their eyes scanning the ground for movement. Sometimes snowy owls will crouch on a small mound of snow and wait, completely still, for prey to wander by. The sound of the jets doesn't seem to faze them at all.

Cars and trucks lumber noisily over big city bridges. But underneath, hidden among the beams and girders, peregrine falcons have found a home. Sleekly built with powerful wings, the falcon is one of the fastest birds on earth. In the city it soars high above the bridges and buildings, hunting for pigeons and small birds flying below. When it spots its prey, the falcon folds its wings tight against its body and dives straight down at speeds of over one hundred fifty miles per hour!

In cities all across the country, people are fascinated with the peregrine falcon and are doing what they can to make this noble bird feel welcome. In many cities people set nesting boxes filled with gravel out on skyscraper ledges. The falcons seem to like these windy, rocky heights, for they return to the boxes early each spring to lay their eggs and raise their chicks. Living on these high perches with no natural enemies and plenty of pigeons, the falcons are adapting well to urban life.

So many birds make their homes in the midst of the city—sparrows and finches, barn owls and snowy owls, nighthawks and killdeers, pigeons and wrens, crows, and falcons. Each has found its own urban roost.

Urban Roosts
Where Birds Nest in the City

Meet the Author/Illustrator

Barbara Bash began her love of art through her love of letters. *"My first connection to art and creativity was through the alphabet. I loved to draw the twenty-six letters. All through elementary school I experimented with their forms constantly."* Her love for art and letters led her to study calligraphy, the art of making fancy letters. From there, she went on to study nature and began learning how to draw it. Her love of nature gave her the desire to create books for children.

Before she writes a book, she learns everything she can about the subject through books, photographs, and films. Then she travels to the area where she can watch the subject. She has gone to Arizona to learn about the cactus and to East Africa to learn about the baobab tree. For this book, Barbara Bash walked through New York City to find where birds make their nests in the city.

Theme Connections

Think About It

Think about what this selection added to your understanding about birds. Here are some things to think about:

- How do city birds have to live with people, cars, pollution, noise, and weather.
- How are these birds' homes like the homes they would have away from cities? Why are these likenesses important?
- What new things about city wildlife have you learned in this selection?

Check the Concept/Question Board to see if there are questions there that you can answer now. If the story has raised any new questions about wildlife in the city, put the questions on the Concept/Question Board. Maybe the next story will help answer the question.

Record Ideas

How is reading a factual article different from reading a story with characters? How is it alike? Write your ideas in your Writing Journal.

Adding Information

Add new information to the classroom chart that you started after the last selection.

The Worm

Raymond Souster
illustrated by Robert Byrd

Don't ask me how he managed
to corkscrew his way
through the King Street Pavement,
I'll leave that to you.

All I know is
there he was,
circling, uncoiling
his shining three inches,
wiggling all ten toes
as the warm rain fell
in that dark morning street
of early April.

Pigeons

Lilian Moore
illustrated by Robert Byrd

Pigeons are city folk
content
to live with concrete
and cement.

They seldom
try
the sky.

A pigeon never sings
of hill
and flowering hedge,
but busily commutes
from sidewalk
to his ledge.

Oh pigeon, what a waste of wings!

Make Way For Ducklings

by Robert McCloskey

Mr. and Mrs. Mallard were looking for a place to live. But every time Mr. Mallard saw what looked like a nice place, Mrs. Mallard said it was no good. There were sure to be foxes in the woods or turtles in the water, and she was not going to raise a family where there might be foxes or turtles. So they flew on and on.

When they got to Boston, they felt too tired to fly any further. There was a nice pond in the Public Garden, with a little island on it. "The very place to spend the night," quacked Mr. Mallard. So down they flapped.

Next morning they fished for their breakfast in the mud at the bottom of the pond. But they didn't find much.

Just as they were getting ready to start on their way, a strange enormous bird came by. It was pushing a boat full of people, and there was a man sitting on its back. "Good morning," quacked Mr. Mallard, being polite. The big bird was too proud to answer. But the people on the boat threw peanuts into the water, so the Mallards followed them all round the pond and got another breakfast, better than the first.

"I like this place," said Mrs. Mallard as they climbed out on the bank and waddled along. "Why don't we build a nest and raise our ducklings right in this pond? There are no foxes and no turtles, and the people feed us peanuts. What could be better?"

"Good," said Mr. Mallard, delighted that at last Mrs. Mallard had found a place that suited her. But——

"Look out!" squawked Mrs. Mallard, all of a dither. "You'll get run over!" And when she got her breath she added: "*This* is no place for babies, with all those horrid things rushing about. We'll have to look somewhere else."

So they flew over Beacon Hill and round the State House, but there was no place there.

They looked in Louisburg Square, but there was no water to swim in.

Then they flew over the Charles River. "This is better," quacked Mr. Mallard. "That island looks like a nice quiet place, and it's only a little way from the Public Garden." "Yes," said Mrs. Mallard, remembering the peanuts. "That looks like just the right place to hatch ducklings."

So they chose a cozy spot among the bushes near the water and settled down to build their nest. And only just in time, for now they were beginning to molt. All their old wing feathers started to drop out, and they would not be able to fly again until the new ones grew in.

But of course they could swim, and one day they swam over to the park on the river bank, and there they met a policeman called Michael. Michael fed them peanuts, and after that the Mallards called on Michael every day.

After Mrs. Mallard had laid eight eggs in the nest she couldn't go to visit Michael any more, because she had to sit on the eggs to keep them warm. She moved off the nest only to get a drink of water, or to have her lunch, or to count the eggs and make sure they were all there.

One day the ducklings hatched out. First came Jack, then Kack, and then Lack, then Mack and Nack and Ouack and Pack and Quack. Mr. and Mrs. Mallard were bursting with pride. It was a great

responsibility taking care of so many ducklings, and it kept them very busy.

One day Mr. Mallard decided he'd like to take a trip to see what the rest of the river was like, further on. So off he set. "I'll meet you in a week, in the Public Garden," he quacked over his shoulder. "Take good care of the ducklings."

"Don't you worry," said Mrs. Mallard. "I know all about bringing up children." And she did.

She taught them how to swim and dive.

She taught them to walk in a line, to come when they were called, and to keep a safe distance from bikes and scooters and other things with wheels.

When at last she felt perfectly satisfied with them, she said one morning: "Come along, children. Follow me." Before you could wink an eyelash Jack, Kack, Lack, Mack, Nack, Ouack, Pack, and Quack fell into line, just as they had been taught. Mrs. Mallard led the way into the water and they swam behind her to the opposite bank.

There they waded ashore and waddled along till they came to the highway.

Mrs. Mallard stepped out to cross the road. "Honk, honk!" went the horns on the speeding cars. "Qua-a-ack!" went Mrs. Mallard as she tumbled back again. "Quack! Quack! Quack! Quack!" went Jack, Kack, Lack, Mack, Nack, Ouack, Pack, and Quack, just as loud as their little quackers could quack. The cars kept speeding by and honking, and Mrs. Mallard and the ducklings kept right on quack-quack-quacking.

They made such a noise that Michael came running, waving his arms and blowing his whistle.

He planted himself in the center of the road, raised one hand to stop the traffic, and then beckoned with the other, the way policemen do, for Mrs. Mallard to cross over.

As soon as Mrs. Mallard and the ducklings were safe on the other side and on their way down Mount Vernon Street, Michael rushed back to his police booth.

He called Clancy at headquarters and said: "There's a family of ducks walkin' down the street!" Clancy said: "Family of *what?*" "*Ducks!*" yelled Michael. "Send a police car, quick!"

Meanwhile Mrs. Mallard had reached the Corner Book Shop and turned into Charles Street, with Jack, Kack, Lack, Mack, Nack, Ouack, Pack, and Quack all marching in line behind her.

Everyone stared. An old lady from Beacon Hill said: "Isn't it

amazing!" and the man who swept the streets said: "Well, now, ain't that nice!" and when Mrs. Mallard heard them she was so proud she tipped her nose in the air and walked along with an extra swing in her waddle.

When they came to the corner of Beacon Street there was the police car with four policemen that Clancy had sent from headquarters. The policemen held back the traffic so Mrs. Mallard and the ducklings could march across the street, right on into the Public Garden.

Inside the gate they all turned round to say thank you to the policemen. The policemen smiled and waved good-by.

When they reached the pond and swam across to the little island, there was Mr. Mallard waiting for them, just as he had promised.

The ducklings liked the new island so much that they decided to live there. All day long they follow the swan boats and eat peanuts.

And when night falls they swim to their little island and go to sleep.

Make Way for Ducklings

Meet the Author and Illustrator

Robert McCloskey learned to play the piano and the harmonica as a boy. He also learned about small engines and inventions. He even thought for a while that he wanted to be an inventor. Then he began drawing and became very good at it. After high school, Robert McCloskey went on to study art in Boston, New York, and Rome, Italy. To prepare for writing *Make Way for Ducklings*, Robert McCloskey bought four mallard ducks to observe and sketch. It took him two years to plan what he wanted to write about and another two to write and draw it. His hard work and patience paid off. He won a Caldecott Medal, an important award for children's books, for *Make Way for Ducklings*. The story is now considered a classic. Robert McCloskey went on to win a second Caldecott Medal, a very rare honor, for his book *Time of Wonder*.

184

Theme Connections

Think About It

What must wildlife do in order to live in a crowded city? Here are some ideas to think about:

- What did Mrs. Mallard have to do to find a good place for her ducklings?
- What does Mrs. Mallard have to do when they are almost run over by the children on bikes?
- How is this fictional story like the factual articles you read?

Check the Concept/Question Board to see if there are questions there that you can answer now. If the story has raised any new questions about city wildlife, put the questions on the Concept/Question Board. Maybe the next story will help answer the questions.

Record Ideas

How did you like this story? Was it fun to read? Why? Record your ideas in your journal.

Write a Story

Write down ideas for a story about city wildlife. Think about *Make Way for Ducklings* and *The Boy Who Didn't Believe in Spring* to see how you can include real information about animals in a made-up story.

City Superheroes

from THE CITY KID'S FIELD GUIDE • by Ethan Herberman

AND NOW A WORD ABOUT RATS

Do you see this circle? It's just wide enough for a rat to crawl through.

Have you touched a cement block? It's just soft enough for a rat to chew.

Have you seen the world's fastest man on television? He moves about as fast as the world's most ordinary rat.

Start collecting facts like these and you soon understand why a famous zoologist called rats "the finest . . . product that Nature has managed to create on this planet." Without question, they stand out among city creatures, mainly by not standing out at all. You can spend hours watching pigeons, but unless you are unusually observant, you may never encounter the rats.

Fat, fat, the water rat! About eight inches long from nose to tail and well-fed, this brown rat (also known as a Norway, water, or sewer rat) belongs to the species most often found in the U.S. But you might also see smaller, black (or roof) rats, usually in high places, when the larger species hasn't driven them away.

186

But that doesn't mean they live someplace else. In big cities they live *everywhere*—in subways, attics, basements and backyards, inside sewer pipes, and underneath wharves. They pop up in people's toilets; they scurry in the shadows of fancy restaurants, sharing dinner with the guests. They live up to their reputation as destroyers of property, spreaders of disease—and the animal superheroes of city life.

They seem to have learned every survival trick in town. Does it help to be "nocturnal"—to be active at night? Well, rats are nocturnal. With their sensitive whiskers they find their way expertly in the lightless spaces between walls. Does it help to be "omnivorous"—to eat a lot of different foods? Well, rats are omnivorous. With teeth that grow nonstop, they gnaw away at everything from grain to pigeons to other rats. Does it help to reproduce quickly? Well, a single female, breeding seven times a year, could theoretically produce 168 new rats during a typical two-year lifespan. Above all, though, these rodents are smart. Consider the

brown rat, for instance, by far the most successful of the two rat species among us. Brown rats have learned a lot since spreading out across the world from their Asian burrows. In the old days, they would swallow almost anything that smelled good. But try poisoning brown rats now. They will barely sample unfamiliar food. And even if you did succeed in hurting one, bad news travels fast! A special chemical called a "distress pheromone" would spread from rat to rat in the victim's tribe, and nobody in that tightly knit family of ten to two hundred members would ever touch your bait again.

So how do we get rid of them—with special poisons expertly applied? That sometimes works, but for long term solutions, most health officials say, "Build them out" and "starve them out": Clean up slums, seal up buildings, put food out of reach. That may seem impossible; but perhaps we had better try, for by now there may be one rat for every two people in the United States. And all together, they destroy about one billion dollars worth of food and property every year.

IMPAWSSIBLE

"But that's impossible," you might say as you pick up the trash strewn all over the yard. "I sealed those cans firmly last night."

Any number of night roamers might have done it: skunks, squirrels, dogs, even your neighbor's cat. But if you really pressed those lids down tight, latched the box, even weighed it down with a heavy rock, then the chances are that the mess was caused by a raccoon.

And chances are it'll be back to do it again tonight.

People seem to have tried everything in their war with these large-brained animals. They've latched chicken coops, and the raccoons unlatched them;

they've sealed up doorways, and the raccoons came in through the chimney; they've hung sacks of bird food on strings from trees, and the raccoons untied—didn't chew through, *untied*—the string.

Despite efforts to deter them, raccoon numbers are booming: More of them wander through some North American communities than ever prowled the same regions before the cities were built. One study turned up 150 per square mile in an Ohio suburb. They're fat, too, as you have probably seen.

Every can is a treasure. A mother raccoon and her cubs dig into someone's garbage. Notice their furry "masks," powerful bodies, and banded tails. About the only items they won't eat are raw onions.

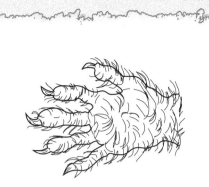

raccoon's forepaw

How do raccoons
pry off lids and untie string?
With sensitive front paws that
look much like a child's hands
and leave similar imprints in
mud and snow.

child's hand

To understand the raccoon's success, follow the next one you see waddling through mud or snow. Don't come too near—don't ever approach or corner a raccoon because it may carry rabies and may bite you. Instead, examine the tracks it leaves behind. Don't the forepaws look like a small child's hands? They are about that sensitive, and what's more, the raccoon is ready to take full advantage of whatever gets within its grasp.

It eats just about everything that comes its way— everything meaning berries, frogs, fish, beetles, breakfast cereal, even kittens. Like the cockroach, it has adapted well to the buildings of humans. In the wild, raccoon nests are often found in hollow trees; but in the city they have been found in sewers, culverts, garages and attics, not to mention the ventilation systems of buildings downtown.

City Superheroes

Meet the Author

Ethan Herberman had a love for science and a talent for writing when he was in school. When it came time to choose a career, he wanted to combine his two favorite interests. He applied for a position as a science reporter at a newspaper. He was on his way. Ethan continued to write about science in children's books and scientific columns. He won the national science writing award in his native country of Canada and awards for his books *The City Kid's Field Guide* and *The Great Butterfly Hunt*.

Theme Connections

Think About It

Would you ever have thought of a rat as a superhero before reading this selection? What new information did you learn about rats and raccoons? Here are some ideas you might think about:

- How are rats and raccoons especially good at adapting to new surroundings?
- Why are these animals thought of as pests? Are raccoons in the wild considered pests?
- What are some of the positive as well as negative things about city wildlife?

Check the Concept/Question Board to see if there are questions there that you can answer now. If the story has raised any new questions about city wildlife, put the questions on the Concept/Question Board. Maybe the next story will help answer the questions.

Record Ideas

Do you think rats are superheroes or super villains? Explain your opinion in your Writing Journal.

Banning Pests

Work with a friend to make a list of ways to keep pests away. Combine your list with your classmates' list to make a class poster.

Raccoon

Mary Ann Hoberman
illustrated by Pamela Carroll

Crash goes the trashcan! Clatter and clacket!
What in the world can be making that racket?
I hurry to look by the light of the moon.
And what do I find? Why, a fine fat raccoon!
All through the garden the garbage he's strewn,
And he's eating his supper, that robber raccoon,
Eating so nicely without fork or spoon,
Why, his manners are perfect, that thieving raccoon!
And wasn't he smart to discover that pail?
And wasn't he smart to uncover that pail?
And isn't he lucky he won't go to jail
For stealing his dinner and making a mess
For me to clean up in the morning, I guess,
While he, the old pirate, abundantly fed,
Curls up in a ball fast asleep in his bed.

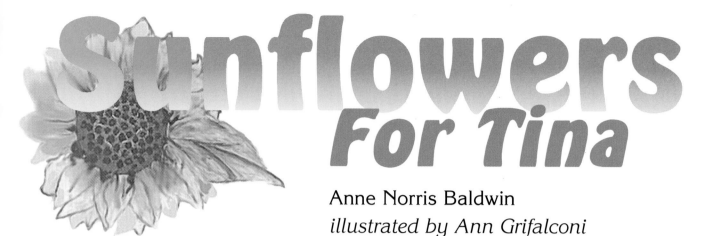

Sunflowers For Tina

Anne Norris Baldwin
illustrated by Ann Grifalconi

ina wanted to grow something. The back yard had a square of dirt that might have been a garden. Nothing grew because no one had planted anything. Behind the square of dirt was a board fence that had once been painted green, and behind that was an alley.

Overhead, the laundry flapped, and sometimes a cat walked the fence, and sometimes Tina's mother leaned out of a window to talk to a neighbor in another window.

Sometimes her brother Eddie drummed on the lid of the garbage can till Tina was ready to scream, and sometimes he didn't because the lid got too hot in summer. Then he and the other boys would turn on the fire hydrant and splash quickly through the cold torrent to cool off before the cops got there.

Tina asked her mother if they could have a garden.

Her mother said, "No. Where'd we have a garden? A garden's a luxury. We're not rich, you know."

"Out back," said Tina, "we could have a garden. There's dirt."

"You just try and grow something in New York City dirt," said Tina's mother.

A block away, Mr. Samuels had his newsstand. He sold cigarettes and candy too, and sometimes he had a few bunches of flowers stuck in a pail of water.

Tina asked Mr. Samuels where he got his flowers.

"From a florist," he said. "I don't sell enough to get 'em from a wholesaler."

"Where do flowers grow?" Tina asked.

"Lord, I don't know. In the country somewheres. In a greenhouse, maybe."

"Don't any grow in New York?"

"I don't think so. I can't think where they would."

Tina had a nickel tied in a handkerchief.

"What will a nickel buy?"

"Life Savers or gum. Most things are ten. 'Less you want to read the news."

"No."

"Life Savers or gum then."

Tina bought cherry Life Savers. When she stuck her tongue out, she could see the Life Saver on it.

Outside his grocery store, Mr. Jones was winding an awning down to keep the sun off the vegetables. The lettuce already looked wilted, but the carrots and onions and radishes were fat and bright as robins.

Tina wanted to ask Mr. Jones if vegetables grew in New York, but he didn't seem to have noticed her standing there. He shook some water over the vegetables and went back inside.

The house sounded very quiet when Tina got home. Her mother was out at work. The upstairs kids weren't there. Eddie wasn't even banging around in the back room. Tina's grandmother sat in her corner of the bedroom, but she never made any noise. She was like a charred old stump, dark and gnarled and bent forever in the same position. Tina wished that she would only say something sometimes. Then Tina would be sure that her grandmother was really alive.

It was going to be a hot day. The kitchen smelled musty. The laundry strung between their building and the next one hung limply. Nothing moved.

Tina looked in the refrigerator. She drank a cool glass of milk and put the carton back on its shelf. It was then that she noticed the bunch of bulging carrots, with tops as fresh and ruffled as Tina's Easter dress. Lush and bounteous gardens sprang into her mind. Acres and acres of greenery grew before her very eyes.

Very quickly and eagerly, Tina untwisted the wire that held the carrots together. She took out half the bunch, and then she put the wire back around the others and replaced them carefully at just their original angle. As she closed the refrigerator door, the hot air from outside rushed back against her face.

Tina took the carrots and a dirty spoon from the sink and went outside. She knelt down on the cracked concrete in front of the little square of earth by the fence, not even noticing that she scraped her knee. The ground was dry and hard. Tina dug at it with the spoon, but she couldn't make much of a hole. The handle of the spoon bent, and she hurt her hand trying to straighten it out.

Tina went inside for some water. The faucet wouldn't stop dripping after she had filled a glass; she gave up and let it drip. She poured the water into the ground where she had been digging and went back for more. The water made digging a little easier. Finally, she was able to bury a stubby carrot altogether.

At last, Tina had planted four carrots in a neat row in front of the fence. The green feathery tops stuck up cheerfully in the sun. She watered them with great and affectionate care.

Tina rinsed the dirt off the spoon and left it in the sink where she had found it. She heard her grandmother moving clumsily in the bedroom, and went to the door. It took a moment for her eyes to get used to the dim light.

"Would you like a drink of water?" she asked her grandmother. It was all she could think of. She considered telling her about the garden, but it didn't seem worthwhile: her grandmother never answered her.

The old lady nodded silently, and Tina brought her a glass. Tina sat down on the floor at her feet. She dug the Life Savers out of her dress pocket, and peeled one off for her grandmother, whose hand shook a little as she took it.

Tina waited impatiently for her mother to come home. From time to time, she went out back and looked at her garden. The day dragged slowly on. The carrot tops began to droop in the hot sun.

From the next yard came the sound of Eddie practicing a tune on his harmonica. Tina hoped that he wouldn't see her garden before their mother did. She was sure Eddie would laugh.

Finally, the gate clicked, and Tina began sweeping the kitchen so that her mother wouldn't see her excitement. Tina's mother came heavily through the back door and began putting away a bag of groceries. Then she washed her hot face at the sink and changed into her slippers. "Phew," she said, wringing her hands. "Summer's here."

Tina danced in a circle around her broom. She did a low curtsy to her mother for fun.

"What's with you, child?"

"Oh nothing. Didn't you notice anything?"

Tina's mother looked all around the room. Then she looked at Tina with a puzzled expression. Tina laughed.

"Give up?"

"Give up."

"My garden!"

Tina swished past her mother and out the door before her mother had time to be surprised. She planted herself proudly in front of the little row of drooping carrot tops and spread out her arms happily toward the sun.

Tina's mother stood squarely in the doorway, her hands on her hips. She stared at Tina.

"What on earth . . .?"

"I planted it myself," said Tina proudly.

"You didn't—!"

"Carrots," explained Tina. "They should grow." But her voice sounded uncertain by the end of the sentence.

"Oh no," said Tina's mother with a look of dismay. "Not our supper. You just dig those right up again!"

The summer went right on being hot and heavy. Even the pigeons looked hot. They waddled lazily around the flat rooftops. Tina's mother swore when they got the laundry dirty.

Eddie got a shoeshine kit from his uncle and spent most of his time hanging around downtown where business was better.

"Why can't you find something to do?" Eddie asked Tina. "Anything's better than just sitting around."

"Like what?"

"I don't know. Help Mom."

"I do."

"You don't."

When Tina started to cry, Eddie felt sorry and said, "Well, don't feel bad. Shinin' shoes ain't no fun either."

"I wish we had a garden." Tina said. She hadn't meant to tell Eddie, but it just came out.

"A garden?" Eddie repeated. "What for?"

"Just to look at. It'd be pretty."

Eddie sat down on the kitchen step. He put the garbage can between his knees and began to drum. He looked thoughtful. Then he said, "I'll be back," and swung through the rickety gate. She could hear him whistling as he loped down the alley.

Later, he came back and said, "I'll show you a garden, Sis," and he jerked his head toward the street.

Tina followed him some three blocks. She felt warmly happy.

Eddie stopped at the edge of an empty lot. "There," he said. "Sunflowers!"

Above them, the side wall of the first building bore the imprint of old walls and chimneys, as if a house had been turned inside out. Once there had been a building instead of the empty lot, and people had lived in it. Now, nothing was left except some broken bricks and crumbled mortar, and the black outline of rooms against the next wall.

Out of the rubble of brick and old cement, two stalks, taller than Tina herself, rose toward the sky. Each one lifted a yellow sun to light the day.

"How beautiful," said Tina. The harsh ruins of the broken building made them seem remarkable. It didn't matter that they weren't her own; they were there for anyone to see.

Eddie started forward to pick them for her.

"No, don't," Tina said.

He hesitated, trying for a moment to understand the expression on her face. Then he shrugged. She heard his penknife click shut inside his hand.

Tina was thinking of something quite different. She had suddenly remembered her old grandmother, hunched and silent in her dark corner, with only the whites of her eyes seeming to move. Her life was dark and old and crumbled, like the empty lot. Tina could only guess what it once had been. There didn't seem to be any sunflowers—any bright spots at all—left in her grandmother's life.

At home, Tina put on her yellow dress. It was almost too small for her, but the color was bright and beautiful against her dark skin.

Around the bedroom she danced. As she twirled, her full skirt filled with air and stood out from her waist, a golden disk of petals.

Tina could feel her grandmother's eyes follow her around the room questioningly.

"I'm a sunflower," Tina said.

Even though the room was very dark, Tina could see her grandmother's whole face crinkle into a smile. The whites of her eyes shone, and her thin shoulders shook under her shawl. Out of the cave between her cheeks came a distant rumble of laughter which Tina had never heard before.

209

Sunflowers For Tina

Meet the Author

Anne Norris Baldwin has written several children's books in addition to the papers she has written as a scientist. First Anne worked as a biochemist. Then after her first child was born, she developed a love for children's books and began writing children's stories. Her love and knowledge of science add realistic detail to her stories.

Meet the Illustrator

Ann Grifalconi illustrates and writes children's books. She has been an artist and a designer. She has also written screenplays for television. Books were important to her as she grew up, and she wants the books she writes and illustrates to have an impact on the children who read them. *"Among other things, my goal is to illuminate* [light up] *either the heart or the spirit or the mind of a child, and hopefully, to bring them something new."*

Theme Connections

Think About It

Many wild things live and grow in the city. Most people who live in cities think it is important to plant flowers and trees around the city. How has your understanding of wildlife in the city changed? Here are some ideas to think about:

- How are plants able to grow on their own? What did the vacant lot have that the sunflowers needed?
- How did Tina's attitude about the sunflowers differ from her brother's? Which one do you agree with?

Check the Concept/Question Board to see if there are questions there that you can answer now. If the story has raised any new questions about wildlife in the city, put the questions on the Concept/Question Board.

Record Ideas

Why do you think the sunflowers made Tina so happy? Write what you thought about Tina and her problem in your Writing Journal.

All About Wildlife

Check the wildlife chart you and your classmates have been making while you read this unit. Is there anything else that needs to be added to the chart?

Bibliography

Backyard Birds of Summer

by Carol Lerner. Everyone likes to feel welcome. Learn how to be a good host to feathered summer visitors.

Backyard Safaris: 52 Year-Round Science Adventures

by Phyllis S. Busch. Someday maybe you'll take a safari on the Amazon, but for now try a few in your own neighborhood. You'll be surprised at what you find.

City Green

by DyAnne DiSalvo-Ryan. With one dollar and a dream, flowers and friendship grow. Read how Marcy transforms an empty lot and a life.

Down to Earth

by Michael J. Rosen. How would you feel about having a backyard garden? This book is full of stories, recipes, and projects to get you started!

The Empty Lot

by Dale H. Fife. Harry, who is about to sell an unwanted empty lot, discovers after close inspection that it's not empty at all.

The Green Truck Garden Giveaway: A Neighborhood Story and Almanac

by Jacqueline Briggs Martin. What happens when two strangers give away almanacs and seeds? Gardens grow, bug tea is made, and neighbors become friends.

Secret Place

by Eve Bunting. There is a mystery in the city between concrete walls. Be one of the few who are in on the secret.

Wild in the City

by Jan Thornhill. The city is alive with more than lights and noise. The night belongs to skunks, raccoons, bats, owls, and other wildlife. Have you heard their voices? Jenny has.

Imagination

Sometimes we are told to stop imagining things. Can we stop imagining things? Should we stop imagining things? How does your imagination work?

The Blind Men and the Elephant

an Indian legend
retold by John Godfrey Saxe • *illustrated by Lane Yerkes*

It was six men of Indostan
   To learning much inclined,
Who went to see the Elephant
   (Though all of them were blind),
That each by observation
   Might satisfy his mind.

The First approached the Elephant,
   And happening to fall
Against his broad and sturdy side,
   At once began to bawl:
"Bless me! but the Elephant
   Is very like a wall!"

The Second, feeling of the tusk,
   Cried, "Ho! what have we here,
So very round and smooth and
sharp?
   To me 'tis mighty clear
This wonder of an Elephant
   Is very like a spear!"

The Third approached the animal,
   And happening to take
The squirming trunk within his hands,
   Thus boldly up and spake:
"I see," quoth he, "the Elephant
   Is very like a snake!"

The Fourth reached out his eager hand,
   And felt about the knee.
"What most this wondrous beast is like
   Is mighty plain," quoth he;
" 'Tis clear enough the Elephant
   Is very like a tree!"

The Fifth, who chanced to touch the
ear,
    Said, "E'en the blindest man
Can tell what this resembles most;
    Deny the fact who can,
This marvel of an Elephant
    Is very like a fan!"

The Sixth no sooner had begun
    About the beast to grope,
Than, seizing on the swinging tail
    That fell within his scope,
"I see," quoth he, "the Elephant
    Is very like a rope!"

And so these men of Indostan
    Disputed loud and long,
Each in his own opinion
    Exceeding stiff and strong,
Though each was partly in the right,
    And all were in the wrong!

The Blind Men and the Elephant

Meet the Author

John Godfrey Saxe was born in Vermont and lived from 1816 to 1887. He was a man of many interests and talents. Saxe earned his living in law and politics but claimed the literary world as his first love. He edited a weekly newspaper and wrote many volumes of poetry. Saxe was one of the most widely read poets of his day and loved to entertain his friends with his humorous verse.

Meet the Illustrator

Lane Yerkes graduated from the Philadelphia College of Art with a Bachelor of Arts degree in illustration. Over the years, he has created illustrations for advertising, newspapers, magazines, textbooks, fabric design, logos, and children's books. Lane Yerkes has written, as well as illustrated, two children's stories that he hopes to publish. His home and studio are located on the southwest coast of Florida, just above the Everglades, where he lives with his wife and their dog. When not working he enjoys boating and fishing.

218

Theme Connections

Think About It

In this unit you will be thinking and talking about imagination. You will read about different ways to use imagination. Here are some ideas to think about:

- Have you and a friend ever had different ideas about what something was even though you were looking at the same thing? How did it happen? What did you decide?
- What do you think the blind men could have done to get a full picture of the elephant?

Check the Concept/Question Board to see if there are questions there that you can answer now. If the story has raised any new questions about imagination, put the questions on the Concept/Question Board. Maybe the next story will help answer the questions.

Record Ideas

 What did you think of "The Blind Men and the Elephant?" Did you like it? Did you think it was funny or silly? Why do you think so? Record your ideas in your Writing Journal.

Try It

How could the blind men mistake an elephant for a snake? Choose an object and place it in a bag or box. Don't let your classmates see the object. Choose a classmate to close his or her eyes and feel the object that you placed in a bag or box. Can your classmate tell what it is? If not, what fooled him or her?

Through Grandpa's Eyes

Patricia MacLachlan
illustrated by Deborah Kogan Ray

Of all the houses that I know, I like my grandpa's best. My friend Peter has a new glass house with pebble-path gardens that go nowhere. And Maggie lives next door in an old wooden house with rooms behind rooms, all with carved doors and brass doorknobs. They are fine houses. But Grandpa's house is my favorite. Because I see it through Grandpa's eyes.

Grandpa is blind. He doesn't see the house the way I do. He has his own way of seeing.

In the morning, the sun pushes through the curtains into my eyes. I burrow down into the covers to get away, but the light follows me. I give up, throw back the covers, and run to Grandpa's room.

The sun wakes Grandpa differently from the way it wakes me. He says it touches him, *warming* him awake. When I peek around the door, Grandpa is already up and doing his morning exercises. Bending and stretching by the bed. He stops and smiles because he hears me.

"Good morning, John."

"Where's Nana?" I ask him.

"Don't you know?" he says, bending and stretching. "Close your eyes, John, and look through my eyes."

I close my eyes. Down below, I hear the banging of pots and the sound of water running that I didn't hear before.

"Nana is in the kitchen, making breakfast," I say.

When I open my eyes again, I can see Grandpa nodding at me. He is tall with dark gray hair. And his eyes are sharp blue even though they are not sharp seeing.

I exercise with Grandpa. Up and down. Then I try to exercise with my eyes closed.

"One, two," says Grandpa, "three, four."

"Wait!" I cry. I am still on one, two when Grandpa is on three, four.

    I fall sideways. Three times. Grandpa laughs as he hears my thumps on the carpet.

    "Breakfast!" calls Nana from downstairs.

    "I smell eggs frying," says Grandpa. He bends his head close to mine. "And buttered toast."

    The wooden banister on the stairway has been worn smooth from Grandpa running his fingers up and down. I walk behind him, my fingers following Grandpa's smooth path.

    We go into the kitchen.

    "I smell flowers," says Grandpa.

    "What flowers?" I ask.

He smiles. He loves guessing games.

"Not violets, John, not peonies . . ."

"Carnations!" I cry. *I* love guessing games.

"Silly." Grandpa laughs. "Marigolds. Right, Nana?"
Nana laughs, too.

"That's too easy," she says, putting two plates of
food in front of us.

"It's not too easy," I protest. "How can Grandpa tell?
All the smells mix together in the air."

"Close your eyes, John," says Nana. "Tell me what
breakfast is."

"I smell the eggs. I smell the toast," I say, my eyes
closed. "And something else. The something else
doesn't smell good."

"*That* something else," says Nana, smiling, "is the marigolds."

When he eats, Grandpa's plate of food is a clock.

"Two eggs at nine o'clock and toast at two o'clock," says Nana to Grandpa. "And a dollop of jam."

"A dollop of jam," I tell Grandpa, "at six o'clock."

I make my plate of food a clock, too, and eat through Grandpa's eyes.

After breakfast, I follow Grandpa's path through the dining room to the living room, to the window that he opens to feel the weather outside, to the table where he finds his pipe, and to his cello in the corner.

"Will you play with me, John?" he asks.

He tunes our cellos without looking. I play with a music stand and music before me. I know all about sharps and flats. I see them on the music. But Grandpa plays them. They are in his fingers. For a moment I close my eyes and play through Grandpa's eyes. My fingering hand slides up and down the cello neck—toward the pegs for flats, toward the bridge for sharps. But with my eyes closed my bow falls from the strings.

"Listen," says Grandpa. "I'll play a piece I learned when I was your age. It was my favorite."

He plays the tune while I listen. That is the way Grandpa learns new pieces. By listening.

"Now," says Grandpa. "Let's do it together."

"That's fine," says Grandpa as we play. "But C sharp, John," he calls to me. "C sharp!"

225

Later, Nana brings out her clay to sculpt my Grandpa's head.

"Sit still," she grumbles.

"I won't," he says, imitating her grumbly voice, making us laugh.

While she works, Grandpa takes out his piece of wood. He holds it when he's thinking. His fingers move back and forth across the wood, making smooth paths like the ones on the stair banister.

"Can I have a piece of thinking wood, too?" I ask.

Grandpa reaches in his shirt pocket and tosses a small bit of wood in my direction. I catch it. It is smooth with no splinters.

"The river is up," says Nana.

Grandpa nods a short nod. "It rained again last night. Did you hear the gurgling in the rain gutter?"

As they talk, my fingers begin a river on my thinking wood. The wood will winter in my pocket so when I am not at Grandpa's house I can still think about Nana, Grandpa, and the river.

When Nana is finished working, Grandpa runs his hand over the sculpture, his fingers soft and quick like butterflies.

"It looks like me," he says, surprised.

My eyes have already told me that it looks like Grandpa. But he shows me how to feel his face with my three middle fingers, and then the clay face.

"Pretend your fingers are water," he tells me.

My waterfall fingers flow down his clay head, filling in the spaces beneath the eyes like little pools before they flow down over the cheeks. It does feel like Grandpa. This time my fingers tell me.

227

Grandpa and I walk outside, through the front yard and across the field to the river. Grandpa has not been blind forever. He remembers in his mind the gleam of the sun on the river, the Queen Anne's lace in the meadow, and every dahlia in his garden. But he gently takes my elbow as we walk so that I can help show him the path.

"I feel a south wind," says Grandpa.

I can tell which way the wind is blowing because I see the way the tops of the trees lean. Grandpa tells by the feel of the meadow grasses and by the way his hair blows against his face.

When we come to the riverbank, I see that Nana was right. The water is high and has cut in by the willow tree. It flows around and among the roots of the tree, making paths. Paths like Grandpa's on the stair banister and on the thinking wood. I see a blackbird with a red patch on its wing sitting on a cattail. Without thinking, I point my finger.

"What is that bird, Grandpa?" I asked excitedly.

"*Conk-a-ree,*" the bird calls to us.

"A red-winged blackbird," says Grandpa promptly.

He can't see my finger pointing. But he hears the song of the bird.

"And somewhere behind the blackbird," he says listening, "a song sparrow."

I hear a scratchy song, and I look and look until I see the earth-colored bird that Grandpa knows is here.

Nana calls from the front porch of the house.

"Nana's made hot bread for lunch," he tells me happily. "And spice tea." Spice tea is his favorite.

I close my eyes, but all I can smell is the wet earth by the river.

As we walk back to the house, Grandpa stops suddenly. He bends his head to one side, listening. He points his finger upward.

"Honkers," he whispers.

I look up and see a flock of geese, high in the clouds, flying in a V.

"Canada geese," I tell him.

"Honkers," he insists. And we both laugh.

We walk up the path again and to the yard where Nana is painting the porch chairs. Grandpa smells the paint.

"What color, Nana?" he asks. "I cannot smell the color."

"Blue," I tell him, smiling. "Blue like the sky."

"Blue like the color of Grandpa's eyes," Nana says.

When he was younger, before I can remember,
before he was blind, Grandpa did things the way I do.
Now, when we drink tea and eat lunch on the porch,
Grandpa pours his own cup of tea by putting his finger
just inside the rim of the cup to tell him when it is full.
He never burns his finger. Afterward, when I wash the
dishes, he feels them as he dries them. He even sends
some back for me to wash again.

"Next time," says Grandpa, pretending to be cross,
"I wash, you dry."

In the afternoon, Grandpa, Nana, and I take our
books outside to read under the apple tree. Grandpa
reads his book with his fingers, feeling the raised
Braille dots that tell him the words.

As he reads, Grandpa laughs out loud.

231

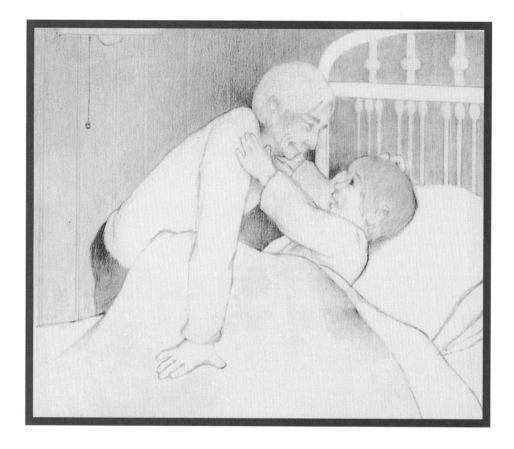

"Tell us what's funny," says Nana. "Read to us, Papa."

And he does.

Nana and I put down our books to listen. A gray squirrel comes down the trunk of the apple tree, tail high, and seems to listen, too. But Grandpa doesn't see him.

After supper, Grandpa turns on the television. I watch, but Grandpa listens, and the music and the words tell him when something is dangerous or funny, happy or sad.

Somehow, Grandpa knows when it is dark, and he takes me upstairs and tucks me into bed. He bends down to kiss me, his hands feeling my head.

"You need a haircut, John," he says.

Before Grandpa leaves, he pulls the light chain above my bed to turn out the light. But, by mistake, he's turned it on instead. I lie for a moment after he's gone, smiling, before I get up to turn off the light.

Then, when it is dark for me the way it is dark for Grandpa, I hear the night noises that Grandpa hears. The house creaking, the birds singing their last songs of the day, the wind rustling the tree outside my window.

Then, all of a sudden, I hear the sounds of geese overhead. They fly low over the house.

"Grandpa," I call softly, hoping he's heard them too.

"Honkers," he calls back.

"Go to sleep, John," says Nana.

Grandpa says her voice smiles to him. I test it.

"What?" I call to her.

"I said go to sleep," she answers.

She says it sternly. But Grandpa is right. Her voice smiles to me. I know. Because I'm looking through Grandpa's eyes.

Through Grandpa's Eyes

Meet the Author

Patricia MacLachlan grew up in a family where reading was encouraged. She and her parents would read and discuss books and then act them out. When she was thirty-five, she began writing children's stories. Her most famous story is *Sarah, Plain and Tall*, but nearly all of her books have received awards and praise. Her concern for families makes its way into many of her books. She says, *"I see that I write books about brothers and sisters, about what makes up a family, what works and what is nurturing."*

Meet the Illustrator

Deborah Kogan Ray loved to play games with the other children in the alley behind the city street where she grew up. *"I was good at games, but,"* she says, *"I felt like an outsider. Mostly I loved to read and draw pictures."* When she was twelve she decided to be an artist. She took extra art classes and went on to college to study art. Deborah began illustrating and writing children's books while raising her two daughters.

234

Theme Connections

Think About It

In this story, we see a blind man finding out about the world through his other senses. John also experiences his grandpa's way of "seeing." Think about how the characters in this story and in "The Blind Men and the Elephant" use their imaginations. Here are some things to think about:

- If you close your eyes, can you "see" your friends? Are you imagining them?
- Can your other senses help you imagine what something looks like?
- Think of a place you have never been but that you have heard about. Can you see it in your mind?

Check the Concept/Question Board to see if there are questions there that you can answer now. If the story has raised any new questions about imagination, put the questions on the Concept/Question Board. Maybe the next story will help answer the questions.

Record Ideas

Why do you think John walked around with his eyes closed? Have you ever tried to feel what someone else was feeling? How did you do it? Record your ideas in your Writing Journal. Remember to use some of these ideas in stories you write.

Do an Experiment

Try John's experiment. Close your eyes or put on a blindfold. Make sure you have a friend or a family member with you so you don't fall and hurt yourself. How do things seem different when you can't see them? What do you smell? What do you hear? How does it feel?

The Apple

Arnold Adoff • *illustrated by Deborah Drummond*

The Apple
        is on the top
branch
        of the tree
                touching
the
sky
        or the apple is
                in
        the
        sky
touching
        the top branch
                of the tree
and i am
        me on the ground
        waiting
                for
                a
        good
        wind

Houses

Aileen Fisher
illustrated by Deborah Drummond

Houses are faces
(haven't you found?)
with their hats in the air,
and their necks in the ground.

Windows are noses,
windows are eyes,
and doors are the mouths
of a suitable size.

And a porch—or the place
where porches begin—
is just like a mustache
shading the chin.

Fog

Carl Sandburg
illustrated by Deborah Drummond

The Fog comes
on little cat feet.

It sits looking
over harbor and city
on silent haunches
and then moves on.

The Cat Who Became a Poet

from *Nonstop Nonsense*
by Margaret Mahy
illustrated by Quentin Blake

Acat once caught a mouse, as cats do.

"Don't eat me," cried the mouse. "I am a poet with a poem to write."

"That doesn't make any difference to me," replied the cat. "It is a rule that cats must eat mice, and that is all there is to it."

"If only you'd listen to my poem you'd feel differently about it all," said the mouse.

"Okay," yawned the cat, "I don't mind hearing a poem, but I warn you, it won't make any difference."

So the mouse danced and sang:

"The great mouse Night with the starry tail
Slides over the hills and trees,
Eating the crumbs in the corners of Day
And nibbling the moon like cheese."

"Very good! That's very good!" the cat said. "But a poem is only a poem and cats still eat mice."

And he ate the mouse, as cats do.

Then he washed his paws and his face and curled up in a bed of catnip, tucking in his nose and his tail and his paws. Then he had a little cat nap.

Some time later he woke up in alarm.

"What's wrong with me?" he thought. "I feel so strange." He felt as if his head was full of colored lights. Pictures came and went behind his eyes. Things that were different seemed alike. Things that were real changed and became dreams.

"Horrakapotchkin!" thought the cat. "I want to write a poem."

He opened his mouth to meow, but a poem came out instead:

"The great Sun-Cat comes up in the east.
Lo! The glory of his whiskers touches the hills.
Behold! the fire of his smiling
Burns on the oceans of the rolling world."

"Cat-curses!" said the cat to himself. "I have turned into a poet, but I don't want to make poetry. I just want to be a cat catching mice and sleeping in the catnip bed. I will have to ask the witch about this."

The cat went to the witch's crooked house. The witch sat at the window with her head in her hands. Her dreams turned into black butterflies and flew out of the window.

She took the cat's temperature and gave him some magic medicine that tasted of dandelions.

"Now talk!" she commanded.

The cat opened his mouth to ask her if he was cured. Instead he found himself saying:

"Lying in the catnip bed,
The flowering cherry over my head,
Am I really the cat that I seem?
Or only a cat in another cat's dream?"

"I'm afraid it is too late," said the witch. "Your case is hopeless. Poetry has got into your blood and you're stuck with it for the rest of your life."

"Horrakapotchkin!" cried the cat sadly, and he started off home.

But, five houses away from his own house, a black dog called Max chased him, as dogs do, and the cat had to run up a tree. He boxed with his paw at Max and went to hiss and spit at him, but instead he found himself saying:

"Colonel Dog fires his cannon
And puts his white soldiers on parade.
He guards the house from cats, burglars
And any threat of peacefulness."

The dog Max stopped and stared. "What did you call me? Colonel Dog? I like that. But what do you mean, I fire my cannon?"

"That's your barking," said the cat.

"And what do you mean, I put my white soldiers on parade?" asked the dog again.

"That's your teeth," said the cat.

The dog wagged his tail. "I like the way you put it," he said again. "How did you learn to talk like that?"

"Oh, it's poetry," said the cat carelessly. "I am a poet, you see."

"Well, I'll tell you what! I'll let you go without barking at you if I may come and hear that poem again sometimes," the dog Max said, still wagging his tail. "Perhaps I could bring some other dogs to hear it too. Colonel Dog, eh? White soldiers, eh? Very true." And he let the cat go on home to his catnip bed.

"If only he knew," the cat thought. "I wasn't meaning to praise him. Poetry is very tricky stuff and can be taken two ways."

The cat went on thinking. "I became a poet through eating the mouse. Perhaps the mouse became a poet through eating seeds. Perhaps all this poetry stuff is just the world's way of talking about itself." And straight away he felt another poem coming into his mind.

"Just time for a sleep first," he muttered into his whiskers. "One thing, I'll never eat another poet again. One is quite enough." And he curled up in the catnip bed for a quick kip-and-catnap, as cats do.

Let's get to the next page before he wakes up...

The Cat Who Became a Poet

Meet the Author

Margaret Mahy was born and raised in New Zealand. She has worked as a librarian and writes children's books. She says that she knew she wanted to write *"from the time I was seven onwards . . . I decided in childhood that I wanted to be a writer, and I used to write in little notebooks, which I also illustrated."* She has written well over 100 books for young readers, as well as several for young adult readers. In her books, she says, *"I try to tell an exciting story, something which children enjoy reading."*

Meet the Illustrator

Quentin Blake was born and raised in England. He is an author, illustrator, teacher, and editor. He has illustrated more than 200 books. Quentin Blake has some words of advice for young artists: *"You must want to draw all the time, because that is the only way you can get good at it. You can study a certain amount of technique, but doing it is the key element."*

Theme Connections

Think About It

You have to use your imagination just to read this story. Can you picture in your mind what is happening? How else is imagination used in this story? Here are some ideas to think about with your group:

- The cat really began to use his imagination after he became a poet. How can you tell that he is using his imagination?
- Look back at the poems "The Apple," "Houses," and "Fog." How are the cat's poems like these poems? How did the poets use their imaginations?
- Look back at "Through Grandpa's Eyes." Were some of the things Grandpa said like poetry?

Check the Concept/Question Board to see if there are questions there that you can answer now. If the story has raised any new questions about imagination, put the questions on the Concept/Question Board. Maybe the next story will help answer the questions.

Record Ideas

Have you ever tried to write a poem? Do you have a favorite poem? Record your favorite poem—either one you wrote or one you just like a lot in your Writing Journal. How did you or the other poet use imagination?

Describe an Object

Pick out one object in the room and write a description of it. Use your imagination. Try to "see" it in a different way. Share your description with your classmates. Can they tell what you are describing?

FINE Art

Cow Triptych. 1974. **Roy Lichtenstein.** Oil on canvas, 3 panels, each 68" × 62". ©Roy Lichtenstein. Photo: Leo Castelli Gallery, New York.

Time Transfixed. 1938. **René Magritte.** Oil on Canvas. 146.1 × 97.5 cm. The Art Institiute of Chicago, Joseph Winterbotham Collection. ©1999 C. Herscovici, Brussels/Artist Right Society (ARS), New York. Photograph © 1996, The Art Institite of Chicago. All Rights Reserved.

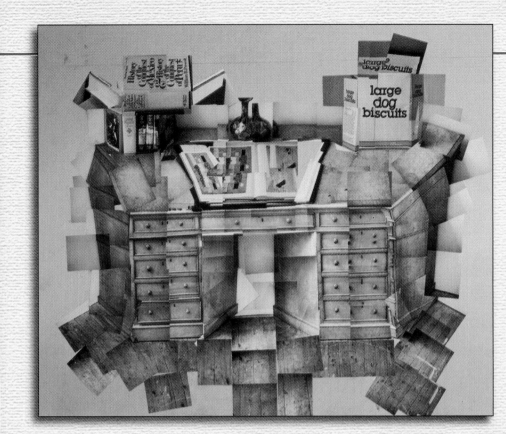

The Desk. July 1st, 1984. **David Hockney.** Photographic collage. $48\frac{1}{2}" \times 46\frac{1}{2}"$. Collection of the artist. ©David Hockney.

Baird Trogon. 1985. **Robert Lostutter.** Watercolor over graphite. 61.5×88 cm. The Art Institute of Chicago. Restricted Gift of the Illinois Arts Council, Logan Fund, 1985. Photograph ©1996. The Art Institute of Chicago. All Rights Reserved.

247

Picasso

from the book by Mike Venezia

Pablo Picasso was one of the greatest artists of the twentieth century. He was born in Malaga, Spain, in 1881, and died in France in 1973.

Picasso's father was an art teacher at the local school. He encouraged his son to paint and draw. He wanted Picasso to become a great artist some day.

Picasso's painting style changed over the period of his life more than any other great artist. He was always trying new and different things.

The painting at the right was done when he was only fifteen years old.

Portrait of the Artist's Mother (Maria Picasso Lopez). 1896. Pablo Picasso.

Oil on canvas. Museo Picasso, Barcelona. ©1999 Estate of Pablo Picasso / Artists Rights Society (ARS), New York. Photo: Giraudon/Art Resource, NY.

Portrait of Dora Maar. 1937. Pablo Picasso.

Oil on canvas. Musée Picasso, Paris. ©1999 Estate of Pablo Picasso / Artists Rights Society (ARS), New York. Photo: Scala/Art Resource, NY.

This painting was done when Picasso was fifty-six.

There's quite a difference between the two paintings, isn't there?

249

When Picasso was nineteen, he left Spain and went to Paris, France. Some of the first paintings he did there look a little bit like the work of other famous French artists.

This painting below reminds many people of the work done by Toulouse-Lautrec. Some of Picasso's other early paintings remind people of Van Gogh, Gauguin, and Monet.

Le Moulin de la Galette. Autumn 1900. Pablo Picasso.

Oil on canvas. Thannhauser Collection. Gift of Justin K. Thannhauser, 1978, Solomon R. Guggenheim Museum. ©1999 Estate of Pablo Picasso / Artists Rights Society (ARS), New York. Photo: David Heald ©The Solomon R. Guggenheim Foundation, New York. FN 78.2514 T34.

The Blue Period

Then something happened! Picasso's paintings changed. His work became different from anyone else's.

His best friend died, and Picasso felt alone and sad. At the same time, none of his paintings were selling, and he was almost starving to death.

Because of his mood, Picasso began to paint with lots of blue (blue can be a very sad color). He made all the people in his paintings look lonely and sad.

Some people thought Picasso's blue paintings were great. Others (including Picasso's father) thought they were just too strange. This meant his paintings were controversial.

The Old Guitarist. 1903. Pablo Picasso.

Oil on panel. 122.9 × 82.6 cm. The Art Institute of Chicago, Helen Birch Bartlett Memorial Collection. 1926.253. ©1999 Estate of Pablo Picasso / Artists Rights Society (ARS), New York. Photograph ©1998, The Art Institute of Chicago, All Rights Reserved.

The Rose Period

Picasso's Blue Period ended when he met a girl named Fernande. Fernande and Picasso fell in love, and soon a happier color started showing up in Picasso's paintings. This was the beginning of the Rose Period.

Not only were Picasso's colors happier during the Rose Period, but he started painting happier things. Picasso painted a lot of circus people during this time. He often painted them with their animals.

The Rose Period didn't last very long, though, because Picasso found a new way to paint that was really exciting and different.

Family of Saltimbanques. 1905. Pablo Picasso.

Cubism

Cubism was the next style of painting that Picasso developed and made famous. The painting on the left is a cubist painting of one of Picasso's friends. The man in the painting looks like he's been broken up into little cubes. That's where the name cubism came from.

Look closely. Can you see the man's face, what he was wearing, his hands, a bottle, a glass, and maybe his pet cat? Can you find anything else?

Cubism is one of the most important periods in the history of modern art.

For hundreds of years, artists tried very hard to paint things so they would look real. Then Picasso came along and started to paint people and things that didn't look the way people and things were supposed to look.

Picasso was always shocking people, but when he started painting people who had eyes and noses in the wrong places—well, even some of his closest friends thought he had gone too far.

Picasso kept working with cubism and changed it over the years. It became much more colorful and flatter looking. It also became easier to see what Picasso was painting.

In the painting below, *Three Musicians*, you can see the three musicians, and tell what instruments they're playing.

Three Musicians. Fontainebleau, Summer 1921. Pablo Picasso.

In another style that popped up for a while, Picasso painted people who looked more real again. Picasso had just visited Rome, a city filled with statues and monuments. When he returned from his trip, he did a series of paintings in which people look like they've been chiseled out of stone, like statues.

Many of Picasso's paintings look funny because of the way he moves eyes, noses, and chins around. The amazing thing about these paintings is how much they look like the real person.

Look at the painting of Picasso's best friend, Jaime Sabartés. Does it look like the same man shown in the smaller painting to the right?

The thing that made Picasso such a great artist was his originality. He had the imagination to try new and different things through his entire life.

Portrait of Jaime Sabartés as Hidalgo. 1939. Pablo Picasso.

Oil on canvas. Museo Picasso, Barcelona. ©1999 Estate of Pablo Picasso / Artists Rights Society (ARS), New York. Photo: Giraudon/Art Resource, NY.

Jaime Sabartés, painted by Steve Dobson, from a photograph by Gilberte Brassai.

Picasso lived to be ninety-two years old. He was a great painter, but he was great at other things, too.

He made sculptures, prints, drawings, beautifully colored dishes and bowls. He even made costumes and scenery for plays.

It's a lot of fun to see real Picasso paintings. You'll be surprised at how big some of them are. Look for his paintings in your art museum.

Most of the pictures in this biography came from the museums listed below. If none of these museums is close to you, maybe you can visit one when you are on vacation.

◆ The Museum of Modern Art, New York, New York
◆ Solomon R. Guggenheim Museum, New York, New York
◆ The Art Institute, Chicago, Illinois
◆ National Gallery of Art, Washington, D. C.
◆ Picasso Museum, Barcelona, Spain
◆ Musée Picasso, Paris, France

Ape and Her Child. 1952. Pablo Picasso.
Bronze. Musée Picasso, Paris. ©1999 Estate of Pablo Picasso / Artists Rights Society (ARS), New York. Photo: Giraudon/Art Resource, NY.

Portrait of Aunt Pepa. c.1895–96. Pablo Picasso.
Oil on canvas. Museo Picasso, Barcelona. ©1999 Estate of Pablo Picasso / Artists Rights Society (ARS), New York. Photo: Giraudon/Art Resource, NY.

Picasso

Meet the Author

Mike Venezia studied art at the school of the Art Institute in Chicago. He thinks the best way for children to learn about art and artists is through fun. *"If children can look at art in a fun way and think of artists as real people, the exciting world of art will be open to them for the rest of their lives."*

Theme Connections

Think About It

This is a different idea of imagination. So far you have read stories about showing your imagination through words and descriptions. This selection is about a real person who showed his imagination through his art. Think about how these ways of showing imagination are alike and how they are different. Here are some ideas to think about:

- Picasso's art changed very much over the years. What does this tell you about his imagination? Has the way that you write or draw changed over the years? How?
- How did Picasso see everyday objects? How can you tell?

Check the Concept/Question Board to see if there are questions there that you can answer now. If the story has raised any new questions about imagination, put the questions on the Concept/Question Board. Maybe the next story will help answer the questions.

Record Ideas

Which of Picasso's art do you like best? What about the art do you like? Record your ideas in your Writing Journal.

Become an Artist

Choose a partner and draw his/her portrait. Pick one of the styles of art that you read about in "Picasso." Draw your partner the way Picasso would. Then let your partner draw you. What style did you pick? Why?

Roxaboxen

Alice McLerran

illustrated by Barbara Cooney

arian called it Roxaboxen. (She always knew the name of everything.) There across the road, it looked like any rocky hill—nothing but sand and rocks, some old wooden boxes, cactus and greasewood and thorny ocotillo—but it was a special place.

The street between Roxaboxen and the houses curved like a river, so Marian named it the River Rhode. After that you had to ford a river to reach Roxaboxen.

Of course all of Marian's sisters came: Anna May and Frances and little Jean. Charles from next door, even though he was twelve. Oh, and

Eleanor, naturally, and Jamie with his brother Paul. Later on there were others, but these were the first.

Well, not really the first. Roxaboxen had always been there and must have belonged to others, long before.

When Marian dug up a tin box filled with round black pebbles everyone knew what it was: it was a buried treasure. Those pebbles were the money of Roxaboxen. You could still find others like them if you looked hard enough. So some days became treasure-hunting days, with everybody trying to find that special kind. And then on other days you might just find one without even looking.

A town of Roxaboxen began to grow, traced in lines of stone: Main Street first, edged with the whitest ones, and then the houses. Charles made his of the biggest stones. After all, he was the oldest. At first the houses were very plain, but soon they all began to add more rooms. The old wooden boxes could be shelves or tables or anything you wanted. You could find pieces of pottery for dishes. Round pieces were best.

Later on there was a town hall. Marian was mayor, of course; that was just the way she was. Nobody minded.

After a while they added other streets. Frances moved to one of them and built herself a new house outlined in desert glass, bits of amber, amethyst, and sea-green: A house of jewels.

And because everybody had plenty of money, there were plenty of shops. Jean helped Anna May in the bakery—pies and cakes and bread baked warm in the sun. There were two ice cream parlors. Was Paul's ice cream the best, or Eleanor's? Everybody kept trying them both. (In Roxaboxen you can eat all the ice cream you want.)

261

Everybody had a car. All you needed was
something round for a steering wheel. Of course,
if you broke the speed limit you had to go to jail.
The jail had cactus on the floor to make it
uncomfortable, and Jamie was the policeman.
Anna May, quiet little Anna May, was always
speeding—you'd think she liked to go to jail.

But ah, if you had a horse, you could go as fast
as the wind. There were no speed limits for
horses, and you didn't have to stay on the
roads.

All you needed for a horse was a stick and
some kind of bridle, and you could gallop
anywhere.

Sometimes there were wars. Once there was a great war, boys against girls. Charles and Marian were the generals. The girls had Fort Irene, and they were all girl scouts. The boys made a fort at the other end of Roxaboxen, and they were all bandits.

Oh, the raids were fierce, loud with whooping and the stamping of horses! The whirling swords of ocotillo had sharp thorns—but when you reached your fort you were safe.

Roxaboxen had a cemetery, in case anyone died, but the only grave in it was for a dead lizard. Each year when the cactus bloomed, they decorated the grave with flowers.

Sometimes in the winter, when everybody was at school and the weather was bad, no one went to Roxaboxen at all, not for weeks and weeks. But it didn't matter; Roxaboxen was always waiting. Roxaboxen was always there. And spring came, and the ocotillo blossomed, and everybody sucked the honey from its flowers, and everybody built new rooms, and everybody decided to have jeweled windows. That summer there were three new houses on the east slope and two new shops on Main Street.

And so it went. The seasons changed, and the years went by. Roxaboxen was always there.

The years went by, and the seasons changed, until at last the friends had all grown tall, and one by one, they moved away to other houses, to other towns. So you might think that was the end of Roxaboxen—but oh, no.

Because none of them ever forgot Roxaboxen. Not one of them ever forgot. Years later, Marian's children listened to stories of that place and fell asleep dreaming dreams of Roxaboxen. Gray-haired Charles picked up a black pebble on the beach and stood holding it, remembering Roxaboxen.

More than fifty years later, Frances went back and Roxaboxen was still there. She could see the white stones bordering Main Street, and there where she had built her house the desert glass still glowed—amethyst, amber, and sea-green.

Roxaboxen

Meet the Author

Alice McLerran has had many jobs and gone to some of the best colleges in the country. She was raised in an army family and says that *"home throughout my childhood shifted every year or so—from Hawaii to Germany, from New York to Ecuador."* In addition to writing, she has worked in the Andes Mountains as an anthropologist and has also been a teacher.

Meet the Illustrator

Barbara Cooney was born in the hotel her grandfather built in New York. Her great-grandfather and mother were also artists, but the only art lesson she received from her mother was how to clean paintbrushes.

She often uses people and images from her own life when she illustrates books. She has won Caldecott Awards, for *Chanticleer and the Fox* and for *Ox-Cart Man.* Barbara Cooney creates art to bring enjoyment to herself and others, and to make the world a more beautiful place.

Theme Connections

Think About It

Imagination doesn't always have to do with fine art. Make-believe games also show imagination. Think about how "Roxaboxen" shows just as much imagination as poems or pictures. Here are some ideas to help you:

- Are you and your friends like the children in "Roxaboxen?" Do you make up games to play? Explain how you use your imagination to make up the games.
- How can a stick be a horse? What does this have to do with imagination?
- How is this story like the story "The Tree House?" What does imagination have to do with both stories?

Check the Concept/Question Board to see if there are questions there that you can answer now. If the story has raised any new questions about imagination, put the questions on the Concept/Question Board. Maybe the next story will help answer the questions.

Record Ideas

 Describe a game you have made up. What was the best thing about the game? Record your ideas in your Writing Journal.

Make a Town

Work with your classmates to create your own town. What would you have in the town? What objects in the room can you use to make houses, stores, and all the other things you find in a town? What will you call your town? Why?

The sun is a yellow-tipped porcupine. . .

Crow Indian Poem
illustrated by Tricia Courtney

The sun is a yellow-tipped porcupine

Lolloping through the sky,

Nibbling treetops and grasses and weeds,

Floating on rivers and ponds,

Casting shining barbed quills at the earth.

The Bremen Town Musicians

The Brothers Grimm
translated by Anthea Bell
illustrated by Josef Paleček

A man once had a donkey who had worked patiently for many long years carrying sacks to the mill, but now his strength was failing and he was less and less useful.

So his master decided to get rid of him, but the donkey, realizing that something was wrong, ran away and set off for the town of Bremen. "I can always join the Bremen Town Band," he thought.

When he had been walking along for a while, he met a hound lying by the roadside, panting as if he had run and run until he was worn out.

"Why are you panting like that, Biter?" asked the donkey.

"Because I'm old," said the dog, "and I'm getting weaker every day. I can't go hunting anymore either. My master was going to kill me, and I ran away. But how am I to earn a living now?"

"I tell you what," said the donkey. "I'm going to Bremen. I'm going to join the Bremen Town Band. Why don't you come with me, and you

can join it too. I'll play the lute, and you can beat the drums."

The dog thought that was a good idea, so they went on together.

Before long they met a cat, sitting by the roadside and looking as miserable as three days of wet weather.

"Well, what's the matter with you, Whiskers, old fellow?" asked the donkey.

"It's no joke when people are out for your blood, let me tell you!" said the cat. "I'm getting old now, my teeth aren't so sharp, and I'd rather sit by the fire and sleep than chase mice, so my mistress was going to drown me. I got away just in time, but now I don't know what to do. Where am I to go?"

"Come to Bremen with us! You're used to singing serenades, so you can be a musician too."

The cat thought that was a good idea, and he went along with them.

Then the three fugitives passed a farmyard. There was the farm rooster, sitting on the gate, crowing for all he was worth.

"Your crowing goes right through me," said the donkey. "What's up?"

"I was forecasting fine weather," said the rooster, "because it's a holiday. But there are people coming to dinner on Sunday, which is

tomorrow, and the farmer's wife has told the cook she wants me in the soup. They're going to cut my head off this evening. So I'm crowing and crowing while I still can!"

"I tell you what, Redcomb," said the donkey, "why not come with us instead? We're going to Bremen. You'll find anywhere's better than being dead. You have a good voice, and if we make music together, it will be a fine noise!"

The rooster liked the donkey's suggestion, and all four of them went along together.

However, they couldn't reach the town of Bremen in one day, and that evening they came to a forest and decided to spend the night there.

The donkey and the dog lay down under a big tree, the cat climbed into its branches, and the rooster flew to the very top, where he would be safest.

Before going to sleep, though, he looked north, south, east, and west, and he thought he saw a little spark burning in the distance. So he called down to his companions to tell them there must be a house not far off, because he could see a light shining.

"Then we'd better get up and go there," said the donkey. "It's not very comfortable here!"

And the dog agreed. A bone or so and a bit of meat, he said, would suit him nicely.

So they set off for the place where the light was. Soon they saw it shining brighter, and it grew larger and larger, and at last they came to a robbers' house, brightly lit.

The donkey, being the biggest, went up to the window and looked in.

"What can you see, Greycoat?" asked the dog.

"What can I see?" replied the donkey. "I can see a table covered with good things to eat and drink, and robbers sitting at it making merry."

"We could certainly make good use of those things to eat and drink," said the rooster.

"Hee haw, I wish we were sitting there!" said the donkey.

Wondering how to chase the robbers out of the house, the animals talked it over, and at last they thought of a way.

The donkey put his forefeet up on the windowsill, the dog climbed on the donkey's back, the cat climbed on the dog's back, and finally the rooster flew up and settled on the cat's head.

When they were ready, a signal was given, and they all began making music together: the donkey brayed,
the dog barked,
the cat mewed,
and the rooster crowed.

Then they crashed through the window and into the room, to the sound of breaking glass.

The robbers jumped up when they heard that frightful noise, thinking a ghost was coming in, and they ran out into the forest in terror.

So then the four companions sat down at the table, set to work on the food that was left, and they ate as if they weren't going to eat again for a month. When the four musicians had finished, they put out the light and looked for a place to sleep, each according to his nature and his notions of comfort. The donkey lay down on the dungheap, the dog lay down behind the door, the cat lay in the warm ashes on the hearth, and the rooster settled on the beam at the top of the ceiling. Since they were tired from their long journey, they soon fell asleep.

When it was past midnight, and the robbers, lurking in the distance, saw that there was no light in the house anymore, and all seemed quiet, the robber chief said, "We shouldn't have let

ourselves be scared like that!" And he told one of his men to go and take a look at the house.

The robber found the house perfectly quiet. He went into the kitchen to get a light, and thinking that the cat's glowing, fiery eyes were live coals, he touched a candle to them, thinking it would catch fire. But the cat was not amused, and leaped for his face, hissing and scratching. The terrified robber ran for it, and tried to get out of the back door. However, the dog was lying there, and jumped up and bit his leg. And as he ran across the yard and past the dungheap the donkey gave him a good kick with his hind leg.

As for the rooster, roused from his sleep by all this noise and wide awake now, he sat on his beam and crowed, "Cock-a-doodle-do!"

Then the robber ran for his life, back to the robber chief, and told him, "Oh, there's a terrible old witch in our house. She spat at me and scratched my face with her long fingers. And there's a man behind the door with a knife, and he stabbed me in the leg. And there's a monster in the yard who hit me with a wooden club. And the judge himself is sitting up in the rafters, and he called, 'Cut the rogue in two!' So I ran for it!"

The robbers never dared go back to their house again. But the four Bremen Town Musicians liked it there so much that they never wanted to leave.

In fact, they liked it better every day, and they all lived happily together in their house for a long, long time.

The Bremen Town Musicians

Meet the Authors

The Brothers Grimm (Jacob and Wilhelm) collected stories that became the fairy tales children around the world have grown up with. "Little Red Riding Hood," "Sleeping Beauty," "Hansel and Gretel," and "Snow White and the Seven Dwarfs" are some of the tales that the Grimm brothers recorded in books. These stories were passed on from mothers and nannies to little children.

The brothers were very close and spent their lives living and working together. "*. . .in our student days, there were two beds and two tables in one and the same room. Later again, we had two desks, still in the same room, and up to the very end, we worked in two rooms next to each other, always under one roof. . .*"

Meet the Illustrator

Josef Palecek loves illustrating children's books. He is also a painter, printmaker, and animator. He says, "*The situation in my country [the Czech Republic] is rather special because many of the best poets write verse for children. These are by no means old rhymes, but true poetry.*" About his work he says, "*I just love working with children—it's fun and bright and full of fantasy.*"

Theme Connections

Think About It

You have read many stories about imagination and how people use their imaginations. You probably use your imagination much more than you think. Sometimes too much imagination is not a good thing. Here are some ideas about the story to think about:

- What do you think of the robbers' reaction to the noise outside the house? What do you think of the robbers' reaction to the animals inside the house? Why?
- Have you ever scared yourself because you mistook something harmless for something frightening? What happened? What did you do?

Check the Concept/Question Board to see if there are questions there that you can answer now. If the story has raised any new questions about imagination, put the questions on the Concept/Quesstion Board. Maybe the next story will help answer the questions.

Record Ideas

The Bremen Town Musicians is a folktale. What other folktales have you read? How did you feel about this story? Why?
Write your ideas in your Writing Journal. Remember to look in your Writing Journal for ideas to use when you are writing.

Bibliography

Behind the Couch

by Mordicai Gerstein. What do you imagine lurks behind your living room couch . . . slippers on the run, living dust balls, your favorite uncle? Find out what Zachary discovers when he searches for his lost toy, Wallace.

Crocodile's Masterpiece

by Max Velthuijs. Are the greatest paintings the ones in museums and artists' studios or the ones in your own mind? Let Crocodile and Elephant help you decide.

The Dancing Man

by Ruth Lercher Bornstein. When he receives a pair of silver dancing shoes, Joseph begins his dance through life. He uses his feet and his imagination to bring joy and courage to the people around him.

Georgia O'Keeffe

by Linda Lowery. Are you a risk taker? Meet a woman who followed her imagination and became a great artist by taking risks and listening to her heart.

How I Spent My Summer Vacation

by Mark Teague. Summer camp getting boring? Carried off by cowboys, Wallace spent his summer vacation in the wild west. Or did he?

Mailing May

by Michael O. Tunnell. Read about May who longs to visit her grandmother 75 miles away. Her parents can't afford a ticket: What great idea gets May to Grandma Mary's by lunch?

My Life with the Wave

by Catherine Cowan and Octavio Paz. A moody friend is hard to get along with. What happens when that friend is a wave?

The Wonderful Towers of Watts

by Patricia Zelver. What does it take to build a dream? Read how Old Sam did it with colored glass bottles, seashells, broken tiles, and his imagination.

281

Writer's Handbook

Table *of* **C**ontents

Grammar, Mechanics, and Usage

Kinds of Sentences 284

Parts of a Sentence 285

Ending a Sentence with the Right Mark 286

Using Commas in a Series 287

Using Commas in Dates and Addresses 288

Using Commas with Beginning Phrases 289

Using Parentheses, Dashes, and Ellipses 290

Using Capital Letters 292

Parts of Speech 294

Using Nouns That Show Ownership 295

Using Pronouns That Show Ownership 297

Using the Right Pronoun for the Right Noun . . . 298

Using Present-Tense Verbs 300

Using Past-Tense Verbs 302

Using Helping Verbs 304

Using the Right Verb for the Subject 306

Using Describing Words
    (Adjectives and Adverbs) 308

Connecting Groups of Words in Sentences 309

Using Negatives Correctly 310

Study Skills

Parts of a Book 312

Using Maps and Charts 314

Using a Dictionary and a Glossary 317

Using an Encyclopedia 319

Reading Directions 321

Library Skills 323

Diagrams 327

Writing and Technology

Using the Word Processor 329

Electronic Tools 331

Finding Information on the Internet 333

Writer's Handbook

Grammar, Mechanics, and Usage

Kinds of Sentences

Rule: A **sentence** is a group of words that makes a complete thought about something. It begins with a capital letter and ends with a punctuation mark.

A **sentence** can tell something, ask something, or show strong feeling. Each kind of sentence ends with a different punctuation mark.

To express your ideas, you need to use different kinds of sentences. You can use the three kinds of sentences correctly by following these rules:

- A sentence that **tells** something is called a statement. It ends with a period.

  Mark read a mystery story.

- A sentence that **asks** something is called a question. It ends with a question mark.

  Do you like to read mystery stories?

- A sentence that **shows strong feeling** is called an exclamation. It ends with an exclamation point.

  That mystery story was so exciting!

Grammar, Mechanics, and Usage

Parts of a Sentence

Rule: Every sentence has two parts: a **subject** and a **predicate**. The subject names the *person* or *thing* the sentence is about. The predicate tells what the subject *is* or *does*. If a group of words does not have these two parts, it is not a sentence.

You need to know how to write complete sentences in order to express your ideas clearly. Using these rules will help you do that.

- Every sentence has a subject. The **subject** names the *person* or *thing* the sentence is about. The subject is underlined in each of these sentences.

  Jean is my best friend.

  Jean and I walk to school together.

  We go to the park after school.

- Every sentence has a predicate. The **predicate** tells what the subject *is* or *does*. The predicate is underlined in each of these sentences.

  Jean is my best friend.

  Jean and I walk to school together.

  We go to the park after school.

Writer's Handbook

Grammar, Mechanics, and Usage

Ending a Sentence with the Right Mark

Rule: Every sentence ends with a mark called a **punctuation mark**—a period, a question mark, or an exclamation point. Writers use these different end marks for different kinds of sentences.

Understanding these rules will help you end each of your sentences with the right punctuation mark.

- If a sentence makes a statement, end it with a **period.**

  Jane has a pet lizard.

- If a sentence asks a question, end it with a **question mark.**

  Would you like to see Jane's lizard?

- If a sentence shows strong feeling, end it with an **exclamation point.**

  I am so afraid of lizards!

Writer's Handbook

Grammar, Mechanics, and Usage

Using Commas in a Series

Rule: In a series of three or more nouns, adjectives, or verbs, use a comma after each word that comes before *and* or *or*.

In a series of three or more nouns, use a comma after each noun that comes before *and* or *or*.

Nouns: My favorite fruits are apples, oranges, and bananas.
Is your favorite color red, blue, or green?

In a series of three or more adjectives, use a comma after each adjective that comes before *and* or *or*.

Adjectives: This apple is big, red, and juicy.

In a series of three or more verbs, use a comma after each verb that comes before *and* or *or*.

Verbs: Mother peels, cores, and slices the apples.

Writer's Handbook

Grammar, Mechanics, and Usage

Using Commas in Dates and Addresses

Rule: Commas are used in dates to separate the day from the year and in addresses to separate the parts of a place name.

In dates, use a comma to separate the day from the year. When you write a date in a sentence, use a comma after the year (except at the end of a sentence).

> **Dates:**
> Abraham Lincoln was born on February 12, 1809. He died on April 15, 1865, a sad day for his country.

Use a comma to separate the parts of a place name. When you write a place name in a sentence, also use a comma after the last word in the place name (except at the end of a sentence).

> **Place names:** Lincoln was a lawyer in Springfield, Illinois.
> Later, he lived in Washington, D. C., the nation's capital.

Grammar, Mechanics, and Usage

Using Commas with Beginning Phrases

Rule: A comma is used to separate a beginning word or phrase from the rest of the sentence.

Readers can sometimes be confused if a writer does not use a comma to separate beginning words or phrases from the rest of the sentence. These rules will show you how to do that.

Beginning words: When a sentence begins with a word that is not part of the main part of the sentence, use a comma after the beginning word.

Yes, I would like to go to the fair with you.
Well, when does the fair begin?

Beginning phrases: When a sentence begins with a phrase that is not part of the main part of the sentence, use a comma after the beginning phrase.

By the way, may I invite my brother to the fair?
In fact, I have already invited your brother to come.

Writer's Handbook

Grammar, Mechanics, and Usage

Using Parentheses, Dashes, and Ellipses

Rule: Parentheses, dashes, and ellipses are punctuation marks. **Parentheses** are used to show extra information within a sentence. **Dashes** are used to show an interruption. **Ellipses** may be used to show a pause in speech, to show an unfinished sentence, or to let the reader know that words are left out of a quotation.

You can use parentheses, dashes, and ellipses to help you express your ideas.

Parentheses: Parentheses are put around extra information in a sentence.

> **We saw a copperhead (a poisonous snake).**
> **We saw a painting by Monet (a French artist).**

Dashes: Dashes may be used to set off a phrase that may break the even flow of a sentence.

> **The triathlon—an event with swimming, running, and bicycling—is demanding.**

In conversation, a dash may be used to show that a sentence was interrupted before it could be finished.

> **"Sharon whispered, "I think I hear—"**

Grammar, Mechanics, and Usage
Using Parentheses, Dashes, and Ellipses (continued)

Ellipses (three dots or ellipsis): Ellipses may be used to show a pause in speech.

"Here are the rose bushes . . . and here are the tulips," Mary said.

Ellipses may also be used to show that a sentence is not finished.

Our garden has tulips, lilies, roses, pansies . . .

Ellipses may be used to show that one or more words from a quotation have been left out.

According to Jones, "There are many species of wildflowers in the world, and about 85,000 species of wildflowers are native to North America."

According to Jones, ". . . about 85,000 species of wildflowers are native to North America."

Writer's Handbook

Grammar, Mechanics, and Usage

Using Capital Letters

Rule: The first word in a sentence always begins with a capital letter. Some words are always capitalized, no matter where they appear in a sentence. Still other words are capitalized only when they are used in a certain way. For example, direction words, such as *east* and *west*, are capitalized when they are part of the name of a place or a street.

- The **first word of a sentence** begins with a capital letter.

  <u>My</u> cousin lives next door.
  <u>She</u> is in my class at school.

- The word **I** is always a capital letter.

  My cousin and <u>I</u> do lots of things together.
  Today <u>I</u> skated with her.

- **Names of people and places** begin with capital letters.

  Abraham Lincoln   Mrs. Myer
  Olive Park   Dallas, Texas
  Tenth Street   Quito, Ecuador
  Dr. Mark Ko   Africa
  Pacific Ocean

Grammar, Mechanics, and Usage
Using Capital Letters (continued)

- **Days of the week and months of the year** begin with capital letters.

    Tuesday, June 14   Monday and Friday
    June, July, and August   the week of May 19

- The seasons of the year *do not* begin with capital letters unless they begin a sentence.

    winter   spring   summer   autumn (fall)

- Words used to show direction are capitalized only when they are part of the name of a place or a street.

    north   east   South Taylor Street
    south   west   West Virginia

Writer's Handbook

Grammar, Mechanics, and Usage

Parts of Speech

Rule: All the words you use are parts of speech. A **noun** names a person, a place, or a thing. A **pronoun** takes the place of a noun. A **verb** names an action or tells what someone or something is, was, or will be. An **adjective** describes a noun or a pronoun. An **adverb** describes a verb.

- A **noun** names a person, a place, or a thing.

  Grandma paints pictures.

- A **pronoun** takes the place of a noun.

  Grandma paints pictures.
  She is an artist.

- A **verb** names an action or tells what someone or something is, was, or will be.

  Grandma paints pictures.
  She is an artist.

- An **adjective** describes a noun or a pronoun.

  Grandma is a good painter.
  She is talented.

- An **adverb** describes a verb. It may answer the questions *How? How often? When?* or *Where?*

  Grandma paints quickly.
  She painted my picture today.

Grammar, Mechanics, and Usage

Using Nouns That Show Ownership

Possessive nouns are used to show who owns or has something. There are **singular possessive nouns** and **plural possessive nouns**. In your writing, you will often need to show ownership.

Rules:

To make a singular noun show ownership, add an apostrophe and s (*'s*).

To make a plural noun that ends in *s* show ownership, add an apostrophe after the *s* (*s'*).

To make a plural noun that does not end in *s* show ownership, add an apostrophe and an *s* (*'s*).

When you want to make a noun show ownership, think about whether the noun is singular or plural. Then use these rules to help you form possessive nouns correctly.

- A singular noun names only one person, place, or thing. To make a singular noun show ownership, add an apostrophe and an *s* (*'s*).

  My cat had kittens.
  My cat's kittens are cute.

Grammar, Mechanics, and Usage

Using Nouns That Show Ownership (continued)

- A plural noun names more than one person, place, or thing. To make a plural noun that ends with an *s* show ownership, add an apostrophe after the *s* (*s'*).

  The kittens sleep in a basket.
  The <u>kittens'</u> basket is next to the stove.

To make a plural noun that does not end with an *s* show ownership, add an apostrophe and *s* (*'s*).

  The geese swim in a large pond.
  The <u>geese's</u> pond is large.

Grammar, Mechanics, and Usage

Using Pronouns That Show Ownership

A **pronoun** is a word that takes the place of a noun. Special kinds of pronouns are used to show who owns or has something. These special pronouns are called **possessive pronouns**. Possessive pronouns are either singular or plural. Here is a list of possessive pronouns:

Singular	Plural
my	our
your	your
his, her, its	their

Rule: Possessive pronouns show who owns or has something. They take the place of possessive nouns.

Noun: Ray's bedroom is always neat.
Pronoun: His bedroom is always neat.

Noun: The girls' bedroom is sometimes messy.
Pronoun: Their bedroom is sometimes messy.

Possessive pronouns are not made with apostrophes. Do not confuse the possessive pronouns *its* and *your* with the contractions *it's* and *you're*. *It's* means "it is." *You're* means "you are."

It's time for the girls to clean their bedroom. Its floor is really dirty.

"Your room is a mess," Mom said. "You're going to have to clean it."

Writer's Handbook

Grammar, Mechanics, and Usage

Using the Right Pronoun for the Right Noun

Rule: **Singular pronouns** stand for one person or thing. **Plural pronouns** stand for more than one person or thing. Pronouns must agree in number with the nouns that they replace.

You must use the right pronoun so that the meaning of your sentence is clear to the reader. When you want to replace a noun with a pronoun, think about whether the noun is singular or plural.

- Use **singular pronouns**, such as *I, me, you, he, she, him, her,* and *it,* to take the place of singular nouns.

    Frank hit a home run today. The crowd cheered for <u>him</u>. His sister Kay waved to <u>him</u> from the stands.

- Use **plural pronouns**, such as *we, us, you, they,* and *them,* to take the place of plural nouns.

    Frank's **parents** could not come to the game. <u>They</u> told <u>their</u> son that <u>they</u> were sorry. "<u>We</u> wish <u>we</u> had seen that home run," <u>they</u> said.

Grammar, Mechanics, and Usage

Using the Right Pronoun
for the Right Noun (continued)

- Use **possessive pronouns**, such as *my*, *mine*, *your*, *yours*, *our*, *ours*, *their*, and *theirs*, to take the place of possessive nouns. Possessive pronouns show who owns or has something. Some possessive pronouns appear before a noun. Some possessive pronouns stand alone.

  Frank's mother is a doctor. His mother is a doctor.
  She owns a computer. It is hers.

Always be sure your readers know exactly to *whom* or *what* each pronoun refers. If it is not clear to which noun your pronoun refers, use the noun again.

Not Clear
Dad bought Frank a new bat. He used it today.

Clear
Dad bought Frank a new bat. Frank used it today.

Writer's Handbook

Grammar, Mechanics, and Usage

Using Present-Tense Verbs

Rule: Use verbs in the **present tense** to show action that is happening now or that happens again and again.

Singular Subject

If the subject of a sentence is *I* or *you*, do not add an ending to the verb.

I <u>make</u> breakfast. You <u>set</u> the table.

For other singular subjects, add *-s* to most verbs.

A puppy <u>sleeps</u>. It <u>dreams</u>.
Its head <u>moves</u> back and forth.

Some verbs have special rules when used with a singular subject:

- If the verb ends with *ch*, *sh*, *s*, *x*, or *z*, add *-es* to the verb.

    A bee <u>buzzes</u>. The puppy <u>dashes</u> under the bed.

- If the verb ends with a consonant followed by *y*, change the *y* to *i* and add *-es*.

    She <u>tries</u> to hide.

Grammar, Mechanics, and Usage
Using Present-Tense Verbs (continued)

Plural Subject

If the subject of a sentence is plural, do not add an ending to the verb.

> Puppies <u>sleep</u> on the floor.
> Sometimes they <u>snore</u>.

Some present-tense verbs have different forms. Pay special attention to them when you write. Here are some examples:

Verb	Present-Tense Forms
be	I <u>am</u>. You <u>are</u>. We <u>are</u>. They <u>are</u>. He <u>is</u>. She <u>is</u>. It <u>is</u>.
do	I <u>do</u>. You <u>do</u>. We <u>do</u>. They <u>do</u>. He <u>does</u>. She <u>does</u>. It <u>does</u>.
have	I <u>have</u>. You <u>have</u>. We <u>have</u>. They <u>have</u>. He <u>has</u>. She <u>has</u>. It <u>has</u>.

Writer's Handbook

Grammar, Mechanics, and Usage

Using Past-Tense Verbs

Rule: Use verbs in the **past tense** to show action that has already happened.

- Add *-ed* to many verbs to put them in the past tense.

  Joy <u>walked</u> home from school and <u>hurried</u> into the house. She <u>laced</u> up her gym shoes. Then she <u>raced</u> outside. She <u>played</u> with Joann until suppertime.

Look at the letters *-ed* at the end of each verb. Here are some special rules to remember:

- If the verb ends with *e*, drop the *e* when you add *-ed*. Notice the verbs <u>laced</u> and <u>raced</u>.

- If the verb ends with a consonant followed by *y*, change the *y* to *i* and add *-ed*. Notice that the verb <u>hurry</u> is changed to <u>hurried</u>.

- For most verbs that have one syllable, one short vowel, and one final consonant, double the final consonant before adding *-ed*. For example:

  They <u>jogged</u> to the park.

Grammar, Mechanics, and Usage
Using Past-Tense Verbs (continued)

Some past-tense verbs have special forms. Pay attention to them when you write. Here are some common examples:

Verb	Past-Tense Forms
be	was, were
do	did
have	had
go	went
come	came
say	said
give	gave

Writer's Handbook

Grammar, Mechanics, and Usage

Using Helping Verbs

Rule: The **main verb** in a sentence tells what the subject is or does. Sometimes a **helping verb** is used with the main verb to show exactly when an action is happening or has happened.

Knowing how to use helping verbs correctly will help your writing to be clearer and more exact.

- Add *-ing* to the main verb when you use the helping verbs *am, are, is, was,* and *were* to show action that is happening or was happening.

  I am looking out the window.
  The boys are playing in the alley.
  The boys were planning their escape.

Notice that if an ending is added to a main verb, you may need to change the spelling, as in *planning*.

- Add *-ed* to the main verb when you use the helping verbs *have, has,* and *had.*

  The boys have climbed the fence.
  The dog had tried this before.

Notice that if a word ends in a consonant and *y*, you change the *y* to *i* before adding *-ed*, as in the verb *tried*.

Grammar, Mechanics, and Usage

Using Helping Verbs (continued)

Rule: Some verbs are called **irregular verbs** because they have special forms. Do not add *-ed* to an irregular verb to show that an action has happened in the past. Here are some irregular verbs that are used with the helping verbs *have*, *has*, and *had*.

Present Tense	Past Tense	Past Tense with *have*, *has*, *had*
do	did	done
go	went	gone
come	came	come
eat	ate	eaten
run	ran	run
see	saw	seen

Writer's Handbook

Grammar, Mechanics, and Usage

Using the Right Verb for the Subject

The **subject** of a sentence is the word or words that refer to the person or thing that performs the action. The **verb** is the word that refers to the action. If you do not use the right form of the verb, you will confuse your readers.

Rule: In a sentence, the verb must agree with the subject.

Regular Verbs

Regular verbs follow this pattern in the present tense:

Present Tense	
Singular	*Plural*
I walk	we walk
you walk	you walk
he, she, it walks	they walk

- Notice that for all subjects except *he*, *she*, and *it*, the verb is the same. For *he*, *she*, and *it*, and for all subjects that can be referred to as *he*, *she*, or *it*, the verb usually takes the ending *-s*.

Maria <u>plays</u> basketball.

Grammar, Mechanics, and Usage

Using the Right Verb for the Subject (continued)

- Verbs that end in -*s*, *x*, -*ch*, *z*, or -*sh* take the ending -*es*.

  He <u>poaches</u> eggs for breakfast.

- In verbs that end in a consonant plus *y*, the *y* changes to *i* before the -*es* ending.

  Marvin <u>fries</u> an egg every morning.

Irregular Verbs

Some common verbs, such as *be* and *have*, are irregular. They have special patterns that must be memorized.

Be: Present Tense	
Singular	*Plural*
I am	we are
you are	you are
he, she, it is	they are

Writer's Handbook

Grammar, Mechanics, and Usage

Using Describing Words (Adjectives and Adverbs)

Rule: An **adjective** describes a noun (person, place, or thing). An **adverb** describes a verb. It may answer the questions *How? How often? When?* or *Where?* Use adjectives and adverbs to make your writing clearer and more interesting.

- An **adjective** describes a person, a place, or a thing.

  The <u>handsome</u> prince married the <u>beautiful</u> princess.
  She is <u>smart</u> as well as <u>beautiful</u>.

- An **adverb** describes a verb. It may answer the questions *How? How often? When?* or *Where?*

  The royal wedding took place <u>today</u>.
  Musicians played <u>everywhere</u>.

Many adverbs are formed by adding *-ly* to an adjective. Notice that the spelling of the word may change when *-ly* is added to it.

  Trumpets played <u>loudly</u>. (loud + -ly)
  The prince and the princess left the castle <u>joyfully</u>. (joyful + -ly)
  They waved and smiled <u>happily</u>. (happi + -ly)
  The crowd cheered <u>wildly</u>. (wild + -ly)

Writer's Handbook

Grammar, Mechanics, and Usage

Connecting Groups of Words in Sentences

Rule: A **conjunction** is a part of speech used to connect words, phrases, or sentences that contain related ideas. The words *but, and,* and *or* are called **coordinating conjunctions**. These words may be used to join sentences or parts of sentences.

Good writers avoid using a lot of short, choppy sentences by using the coordinating conjunctions *and, but* and *or* to join sentences and sentence parts.

■ The word *and* may be used to join two sentences or sentence parts that contain related ideas. Do not use *and* to connect all of your ideas, however.

In my dream, the dragon opened its mouth, <u>and</u> fire came out of it.
In my backpack, I had a carrot <u>and</u> a banana.
I took them out <u>and</u> gave them to the dragon.

■ The word *but* may be used to join two sentences or sentence parts that contain opposite ideas.

I wanted to run away, <u>but</u> my feet felt like bricks.
The dragon ate the carrot <u>but</u> spit out the banana.

■ The word *or* may be used to give a choice or to join sentence parts that give a choice.

I could yell for help, <u>or</u> I could try to make friends with the dragon.
I could run away now <u>or</u> visit with the dragon.

Writer's Handbook

Grammar, Mechanics, and Usage

Using Negatives Correctly

A **negative** is a word that says or means "no." Negatives include words such as *not, no, never, nobody, none, nothing, isn't,* and *doesn't.*

> The mail is <u>not</u> here yet. It <u>never</u> comes before noon. Yesterday there was <u>nothing</u> interesting in the mail. <u>Nobody</u> has written to me for a long time.

Here are some **contractions** that are made with a verb and the word *not.* They are also negatives.

Verb	+	Not	=	Contraction
is	+	not	=	isn't
are	+	not	=	aren't
can	+	not	=	can't
will	+	not	=	won't
could	+	not	=	couldn't

Grammar, Mechanics, and Usage
Using Negatives Correctly (continued)

Rule: Be sure that the subject agrees with the verb in any contractions you use.

Incorrect

He don't get mail.

(He and do not do not agree.)

Correct

He doesn't get mail.

(He and does not do agree.)

Rule: Use only one negative in a single sentence. Do not use double negatives.

Double Negative

I never get no mail.

(This says that there is never a time when I get no mail. This is not what I really wanted to say.)

Correct

I never get any mail.

Writer's Handbook

Study Skills

Parts of a Book

The main part of a book is where the author tells a story or gives information, but books also have other parts. All books have a title page and a copyright page. Some books also have a table of contents, a glossary, a bibliography, and an index.

If you know the parts of a book and how to use them, you can easily find out the information you need, what the book is about, on which pages stories or articles begin, and the meanings of words that you do not understand.

The Front of the Book

The title page, copyright page, and table of contents are at the front of the book.

- The **title page** gives the title of the book, the name of the author or editor, and the name of the publisher.

- The **copyright page** comes after the title page. It gives the publisher's name and the place and year in which the book was published.

- The **table of contents** is a list, in order of appearance, of the units, chapters, or stories in the book, along with the page number on which each begins.

Study Skills
Parts of a Book (continued)

The Back of the Book

The glossary, bibliography, and index are at the back of the book. Sometimes a bibliography is placed at the end of each chapter or unit.

- The **glossary** is an alphabetical list of new words that are used in the book, along with their definitions.

- The **bibliography** is an alphabetical list of other books that the author of the book used to find information. It may also include other writings that the author thinks would interest the reader.

- The **index** is an alphabetical list of names, places, and topics covered in the book, with the numbers of the pages on which they are mentioned or discussed.

Study Skills

Using Maps and Charts

Maps are drawings that show where places such as cities, states, and countries and things such as rivers, mountains, oceans, and parks are located. Symbols and colors are used to show the information on maps.

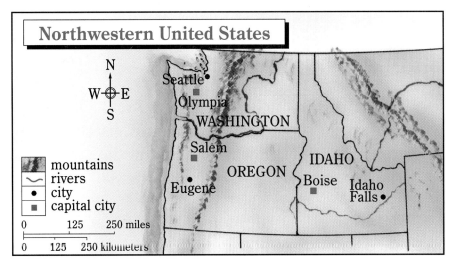

- The **title** of a map tells what information the map shows. The map on this page is a map of the northwestern United States that shows features such as rivers, mountains, and cities.

- The **key** of a map explains what each special symbol or color on the map stands for. Here are some symbols used on the map on this page:

- Maps are much smaller than the places they show. The **scale** on a map shows how the distance on the map relates to distance on real land.

Study Skills
Using Maps and Charts (continued)

- **Direction arrows** show north, south, east, and west on the map. North is usually toward the top of a map. This means that south is toward the bottom, east is to the right, and west is to the left.

Charts can present a lot of information in a small amount of space. Information is often listed in columns and rows to help readers find specific information.

Favorite Lunch Box Foods			
Class	*Sandwich*	*Fruit*	*Drink*
Grade 1	peanut butter	banana	milk
Grade 2	bologna	apple	apple juice
Grade 3	turkey	**orange**	milk

- The **title** of a chart tells what the chart is about.

- The items for which information is being given are listed down the left side of the chart. These headings are called **row headings**.

- Short headings across the top of the chart tell the kinds of information being given about each item. These are called **column headings**.

- Lines between the rows and columns make the chart easy to read. The lines form boxes that contain brief information about the items in the headings.

Study Skills

Using Maps and Charts (continued)

To find specific information about an item in a chart:

1. Look at the left side of the chart to find the row heading for that item.

2. Then, look in that row for the box that is under the column heading for the information you want.

■ To find the favorite lunch box fruit for Grade 3, first find the row **Grade 3**, then look across the row to the box in the column **Fruit**. The box tells you that the favorite lunch box fruit for Grade 3 is an orange.

Writer's Handbook

Study Skills

Using a Dictionary and a Glossary

A **dictionary** is a book that tells the meaning of most words that people use when they speak, read, and write.

- The words in a dictionary are listed in ABC order and in dark type. These words are called **entry** words.

- At the top of each dictionary page are two words printed in dark type called **guide words**. The word on the left is the first entry word on the page. The word on the right is the last entry word on the page. All other words on the page fall in ABC order between the two guide words. Guide words help you find the page on which the word you are looking for is listed.

Dictionaries can help you understand new words you find in your reading. A dictionary is also helpful when you proofread your writing. Here is how the entry word *garment* might look in a dictionary:

garment (gär′ mənt) *n.* An article of clothing.

Study Skills
Using a Dictionary and a Glossary (continued)

Information about the entry word is printed in lighter type after the word. The information tells how the word is pronounced (gär´ mənt), what part of speech it is (*n.*) and what its meaning or meanings are.

A **glossary** is a section in the back of a book that gives the meanings of certain words that appear in the book. Sometimes these words have special meanings. Here is how the word *flat* might look in a book about plays:

> **flat:** a wooden frame covered with cloth used as part of the scenery in a play

Study Skills

Using an Encyclopedia

An **encyclopedia** is one or more books that contain information on many subjects. Each book in a set is called a **volume** and is marked with a letter or a number to show what subjects are inside.

Encyclopedias are a good place to begin looking for information about almost any subject. Here are some guidelines for using an encyclopedia:

- The subjects within an encyclopedia are usually arranged in ABC order.

- When you want to use an encyclopedia, look up your subject in the **index**. The index will list the articles with information about your subject.

- Find the key word or words of your subject in the index. For example, if you wanted to find out how wounded soldiers were cared for during the Civil War, you would look up the words *Civil War* in the index of the encyclopedia.

If you are looking up information about a person, it will be listed under that person's last name. For example, the entry for Clara Barton would look like this:

Barton, Clara

Study Skills
Using an Encyclopedia (continued)

■ From the index, make a list of articles that have information on your subject. After each article's title, you will find the volume number or letter, a colon (:), and then the page number. Copy this information to help you find the articles. Sometimes an index entry also names other articles in the encyclopedia with information about that subject:

Barton, Clara 2:407; 15:326
  American Red Cross 1:265
  Civil War, in the 4:325

■ Choose the encyclopedia volumes that you need. Turn to the suggested pages and find each article. Browse through each article and write down in your own words the most important information.

■ Sometimes other articles that have information about your subject are listed at the end of an article:

see also American Red Cross

Finally, a list of books with more information about your subject may be given at the end of an article.

Writer's Handbook

Study Skills

Reading Directions

Directions tell you what to do or how to do something. You will need to read and follow directions for many different reasons, such as taking tests, completing assignments or activities, playing games, using new things, and going to a new place.

Here are the steps you should take when reading and following directions:

- Carefully read all of the directions.

  When reading directions, look for key words such as *start*, *first*, *next*, *before*, *then*, and *finally*. These will help you to understand the order of the steps you need to take.

  Also look for key words such as *remember*, *always*, and *never*. These words point out important things to keep in mind while following the directions.

  It is also important to be aware of action words that tell you what to do, such as *write*, *draw*, *choose*, *think*, *look*, *say*, *turn*, and *stop*.

- Check to be sure that you understand the directions by trying to visualize the steps involved.

  If you find that you are unsure of what to do in any step, reread the directions until you understand them.

Study Skills
Reading Directions (continued)

If, after rereading, you still have trouble understanding any part of the directions, ask questions of classmates or ask a teacher to help you understand.

- Follow the directions in the order they were given.

When you are done, check to be sure that you followed the directions correctly. You can do this by rereading the directions, by comparing your results with those of your classmates, or by asking a teacher.

Writer's Handbook

Study Skills

Library Skills

The **library** is a good place to start doing research on a particular topic. It has many different sources of information on many subjects.

- An **atlas** is a book of maps with information about continents, countries, states, cities, oceans, rivers, and mountains.

- An **encyclopedia** is a set of books that contain information on many subjects. For more information about using an encyclopedia, see **Using an Encyclopedia**, page 319.

- **Magazines** and **newspapers** contain many facts. You can get the most up-to-date information from them.

- A **nonfiction book** presents facts on a topic. You may read the entire book or take information from a few pages.

The **card catalog** or **computer catalog** contains information about the books in a library. Some libraries list books on file cards that are stored in small drawers. Other libraries have the catalog of books on computer files. Both catalogs provide the same information.

Knowing how to use the card catalog or computer catalog can help you find library books on your subject quickly.

Study Skills
Library Skills (continued)

- There are three types of cards. The **author card** lists the author's name at the top. The **title card** lists the book's title at the top. The **subject card** lists the subject of the book at the top.

- The **call number** in the top left-hand corner of each card helps you find on which shelf the book belongs. Matching the number of the card to the numbers on the shelves helps you find the book.

- Each card names the publishing company and tells when and where the book was published. Check the date that the book was published to see if the information is up-to-date.

- Each card also tells how many pages the book has and whether it has illustrations. The number of pages can give you an idea of how much information is in the book.

- Each card gives a summary of the book. The summary can help you decide whether the book has the information you need.

Study Skills
Library Skills (continued)

The ***Children's Magazine Guide*** lists articles that have been published in many children's magazines. The guides are published once a month. They are found in the reference section or children's section of the library. Using the *Children's Magazine Guide* can help you find magazine articles with up-to-date information for your research.

Here are features of the *Children's Magazine Guide* that you should know:

- The front cover shows the month or months when the articles listed in the guide were published.

- In the front of the guide is a list of abbreviations used in the guide. They stand for the names of magazines and often-used terms.

  Child D—CHILDREN'S DIGEST
  p—page(s)

- The guide is arranged alphabetically by subject headings. Each heading is followed by a list of articles. After the article title is the author's name, the name of the magazine, the date of the magazine, and the page numbers of the article in the magazine. Sometimes an author's name is not listed.

  TOYS
  FreeTalk Two-way Radio. *Girls' Life.*
      Dec–Jan '98 p32
  1997 Toy Test. *Zillions* Nov–Dec '97 p12–15

Study Skills
Library Skills (continued)

- Some subject headings will tell you to look under a different subject for information.

BUGS: *see* Insects
REPTILES: *see also* Snakes

There are many different sources of information in a library. Knowing where to look for information and how to find it will help you in your research.

Writer's Handbook

Study Skills

Diagrams

A **diagram** is a plan, drawing, or outline that shows how something works, that labels or explains the parts of something, or that shows the relationship between the parts of something.

- The **title** of a diagram tells what information the diagram shows. The diagram below is of the human tongue. It shows the location of the different types of taste buds on the tongue.

- Items on the diagram are labeled. Often, these **labels** include additional information to help you understand the diagram. Sometimes items are labeled with numbers, and then, the numbered items are named below the picture.

THE TONGUE

The Taste Buds

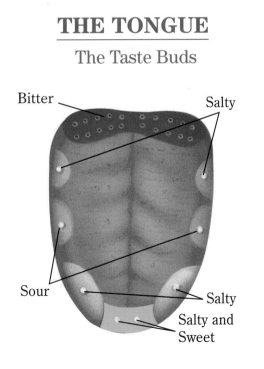

Bitter
Salty
Sour
Salty
Salty and Sweet

Study Skills
Diagrams (continued)

- If a diagram shows a cycle or process, arrows will show the steps or stages of the cycle. Often, there are additional notes near these arrows to show what occurs at each stage.

THE EAR

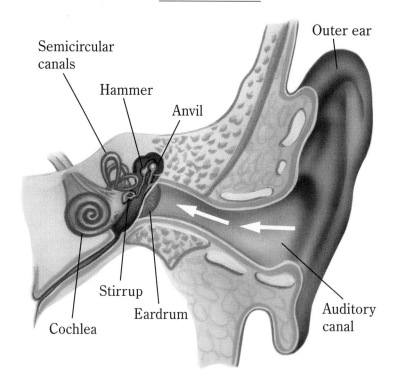

Writing and Technology

Using the Word Processor

A **word processor** is a computer program that allows you to create, edit, and save your writing. Using a word processor for your writing can save time, help make your writing better, and make it easier for others to read your writing.

A word processor has features that an ordinary typewriter does not have, such as **delete, cut, copy,** and **paste,** a **spelling checker,** and a **thesaurus**. Knowing how to use these features will make it easier for you to revise and edit your writing to make it better.

- The **delete** key allows you to back up and erase what you have written. This is useful when you change your mind about what you want to write, when you have made an error in spelling or typing, or when you have made any other kind of mistake that you want to correct.

- You can use the **cut, paste,** and **copy** features of a word processor to revise and edit your work neatly and efficiently. You can copy a word, sentence, paragraph, or entire page to use in the same document or in another document without having to retype. You can move or insert text by cutting or copying it and then pasting it wherever you want it in the document.

Writing and Technology
Using the Word Processor (continued)

■ A word processor's **spelling checker** is a fast and easy way to check for misspellings in your writing. For more information about using a spelling checker, see **Electronic Tools** on the next page.

■ Many word-processing programs include a **thesaurus** that helps you find synonyms for a word you have used. For more information on using an electronic thesaurus, see **Electronic Tools** on the next page.

A word processor has other advantages, including the save and print features and the ability to easily share documents in several ways.

Save: Saving a document on the computer allows you to come back and work on it or read it at a later time. Your work is easier to organize and takes up less space when it has been saved on a computer.

Print: Any number of copies of a saved document can be printed out at any time.

Share: Your document can be easily shared with others by sending it over the Internet or by putting it on a disk.

Writer's Handbook

Writing and Technology

Electronic Tools

Word processing programs have a **spelling checker.** It will find a group of letters that is not in the dictionary and then ask you if you wish to keep this spelling or change it. It will usually suggest the correct spelling.

In the sample below, the word *please* is misspelled.

```
┌──────────────────── Spelling ────────────────────┐
│ ■                                                 │
│ Not in Dictionary: pleese                         │
│                                                   │
│ Change To:   │ please              │  ┌─Ignore─┐ ┌─Ignore All─┐ │
│ Suggestions: │ please          ⬆  │  ┌─Change─┐ ┌─Change All─┐ │
│              │ pleas           ▓  │                            │
│              │ plisse          ▓  │  ┌──Add───┐ ┌───Close────┐ │
│              │ plies           ⬇  │  ┌Suggest─┐ ┌─Options...─┐ │
│ Add Words To: │ <NONE>         ▼  │                            │
└───────────────────────────────────────────────────┘
```

When using an electronic spelling checker, remember the following:

- The spelling checker cannot tell you if you have used an incorrect homonym. For example, you must still check words such as *to, too, two; their, they're, there;* and *sale, sail.*

- If a misspelled word results in the correct spelling of another word, the spelling checker will not point it out for you. For example, if you misspell the word *them* as *then*, the computer will not recognize this as a misspelled word.

- Even if you have a spelling checker, you must still proofread what you have written.

Writing and Technology

Electronic Tools (continued)

A **thesaurus** offers one or more synonyms for a word. A synonym is a word with the same or nearly the same meaning as another word.

To use the thesaurus, you must indicate the word you wish to replace. If the word has several meanings or can be used as more than one part of speech, the thesaurus will indicate the meaning or part of speech and offer possible synonyms. In the sample below, a student has asked for synonyms for the word *break*.

```
┌─────────────────────────────────────────────────────────┐
│▒▒▒▒▒▒▒▒▒▒▒▒▒▒▒▒▒▒▒▒▒ Thesaurus ▒▒▒▒▒▒▒▒▒▒▒▒▒▒▒▒▒▒▒▒▒│
├─────────────────────────────────────────────────────────┤
│ Replace:   break                      [Replace] [Original]│
│                                                           │
│ With:    │break              │  [▼]  [Look Up] [Cancel]  │
│                                                           │
│ Meanings For: break            Synonyms:                  │
│ ┌──────────────────────┬─┐    ┌──────────────────────┬─┐ │
│ │fracture (noun)       │⇧│    │cleft                 │⇧│ │
│ │quarrel (noun)        │ │    │crack                 │ │ │
│ │pause (noun)          │ │    │rift                  │ │ │
│ │breach (noun)         │ │    │split                 │ │ │
│ │respite (noun)        │ │    │tear                  │ │ │
│ │destroy (verb)        │ │    │rupture               │ │ │
│ │violate (verb)        │ │    │division              │ │ │
│ │dissolve (verb)       │ │    │                      │ │ │
│ │injure (verb)         │⇩│    │                      │⇩│ │
│ └──────────────────────┴─┘    └──────────────────────┴─┘ │
└─────────────────────────────────────────────────────────┘
```

When using an electronic thesaurus, remember:

- Not all synonyms have the same meaning. Choose the word that most closely matches the meaning you want.

- Words such as *break* can be either nouns or verbs. Always replace a word with another word that is the same part of speech.

Writer's Handbook

Writing and Technology

Finding Information on the Internet

The **Internet** is an excellent source of information on any topic. The Internet consists of a vast number of web sites and web pages on related topics.

The best way to begin looking for information on the Internet is to use a **search engine.**

A search engine usually offers two general options for searching on the Internet:

- You can search the entire Internet, or you can search certain areas of the Internet for specific information. For this type of search, you enter a keyword or subject.

  For example, if you are looking for information about camping in national parks, you can search the Internet for *national parks*. You may need to narrow your search several times. In this case, you might try searching within your original search results by entering *camping* or the name of a specific national park, such as *Yellowstone*.

- Many search engines also offer **areas** to search. These areas are collections of web sites and web pages that the managers of the search engine have chosen because these sites and pages contain useful information about a particular topic.

Writing and Technology

Finding Information on the Internet (continued)

For example, if you want to find information about a well-balanced diet, try looking in the search engine's *Health* area. This will usually be a collection of useful sites related to all areas of health, including nutrition. Browsing through these sites may help you find more specific, useful information about your topic. Depending on your subject, you may look in other areas, such as *Travel* or *Education*, that will help you find information.

The areas chosen by search-engine managers may also include a *Research* area, which you may find very helpful. Research areas may include on-line encyclopedias, atlases, magazines, newspapers, dictionaries, homework help sites, and other types of research resources. Follow the instructions at these sites to find useful information.

335

Glossary

A

abandon (ə ban´ dən) *v.* To leave empty.

absorb (ab sorb´) *v.* To soak up.

abundantly (ə bun´ dənt lē) *adv.* With more than enough; richly; well.

abuse (ə byo͞os´) *n.* Unkind or cruel words or actions.

acre (ā´ kər) *n.* An amount of land that is about one-third of a city block in size; 43,560 square feet.

adapt (ə dapt´) *v.* To fit in.

adequate (ad´ i kwit) *adj.* As much as needed; enough.

adorn (ə dorn´) *v.* To decorate.

affectionate (ə fek´ shə nit) *adj.* Friendly; loving.

ailanthus tree (ā lan´ thəs trē´) *n.* A wide-spreading tree with long leaves and thick clusters of flowers.

amber (am´ bər) *n.* A yellowish-brown color.

amethyst (am´ ə thist) *n.* A purple color.

amuse (ə myo͞oz´) *v.* To please.

ao dai (ow zī) *n. Vietnamese.* A garment worn by females in Vietnam, usually for special occasions.

> **Pronunciation Key: a**t; l**ā**te; c**â**re; f**ä**ther; s**e**t; m**ē**; **i**t; k**ī**te; **o**x; r**ō**se; **ô** in b**ou**ght; c**oi**n; b**oo**k; t**oo**; f**o**rm; **ou**t; **u**p; **u**se; t**û**rn; **ə** sound in **a**bout, chick**e**n, penc**i**l, cann**o**n, circ**u**s; **ch**air; **hw** in **wh**ich; ri**ng**; **sh**op; **th**in; t**h**ere; **zh** in trea**s**ure.

apathetic (ap´ ə thet´ ik) *adj.* Not interested; not caring about something.

aphid (ā´ fid) *n.* A tiny insect that lives on the juice of plants.

approach (ə prōch´) *v.* To come near.

arctic (ärk´ tik) *adj.* Having to do with the area around the North Pole.

auburn (ô´ bərn) *adj.* Reddish-brown.

audible (ô´ də bəl) *adj.* Loud enough to be heard.

awning (ô´ ning) *n.* A canvas cover for a door or window to shade the sun.

B

baby-sitter (bā´ bē sit´ ər) *n.* A person who takes care of a child when the child's parents are not home.

bandit (ban´ dit) *n.* A robber; a thief.

banister (ban´ ə stər) *n.* The railing on a staircase.

barbed (bärbd) *adj.* With a sharp point.

bawl (bôl) *v.* To yell loudly; to cry out.

beckon (bek´ ən) *v.* To invite someone by waving.

biologist (bī ol´ ə jist) *n.* A person who studies plants and animals.

blunt (blunt) *adj.* Having a dull or thick edge.

bolster (bōl´ stər) *v.* To support; to make stronger.

bounteous (boun´ tē əs) *adj.* Full; plentiful.

Braille (brāl) *n.* A system of printing with raised dots that stand for letters. Blind people read Braille by touching the dots.

breadbox (bred´ boks´) *n.* A special box for keeping bread fresh.

bridle (brīd´ l) *n.* The part of a horse's harness that goes over its head.

burdock (bûr´ dok) *n.* A weed with coarse, broad leaves and prickly heads or burs.

C

camouflage (kam´ ə fläzh´) *v.* To disguise; to hide.

canopy (kan´ ə pē) *n.* An overhead covering.

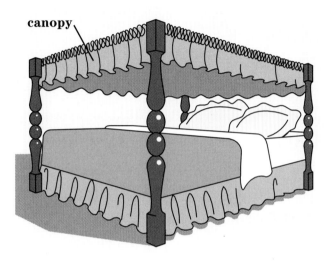
canopy

cartwheel (kärt´ hwēl´) *n.* A jump made by landing on the hands and then the feet, turning like a wheel.

cast (kast) *v.* To throw.

catnip (kat´ nip) *n.* A spicy-smelling plant that cats like.

cavity (kav´ i tē) *n.* A small hole; a hollow.

chant (chant) *v.* To sing or repeat words as a group.

chao buoi sang (chow bwē sung) *Vietnamese.* Good morning.

charred (chärd) *adj.* Burned-looking.

chisel (chiz´ əl) *v.* To cut with a metal tool.

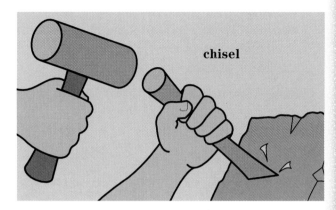
chisel

chive (chīv) *n.* A small plant related to leeks and onions.

circulate (sûr´ kyə lāt´) *v.* To pass around.

clamor (klam´ ər) *n.* A loud, lengthy noise.

clutch (kluch) *n.* A group of eggs to be hatched.

coax (kōks) *v.* To encourage.

colonel (kûr´ nl) *n.* An officer in the army, marines, or air force.

commotion (kə mō´ shən) *n.* A disturbance; a fuss; a lot of noise and confusion.

commute (kə myoot´) *v.* To travel between two places every day.

companion (kəm pan´ yən) *n.* A friend; someone who goes along or in company with someone else.

compete (kəm pēt´) *v.* To try to win by striving against another person or people.

D

complex (kom´ pleks) *n.* A group of related things.

content (kən tent´) *adj.* Satisfied; pleased.

controversial (kon´ trə vûr´ shəl) *adj.* Causing arguments or different opinions.

corkscrew (kork´ skroo´) *v.* To move by turning back and forth or twisting.

cranny (kran´ ē) *n.* A slit; a narrow opening.

creed (krēd) *n.* The statement of a person's belief or faith.

crevice (krev´ is) *n.* A crack.

crinkle (kring´ kəl) *v.* To wrinkle.

crouch (krouch) *v.* To bend down with knees bent.

cubism (kyoo´ biz əm) *n.* A style of painting in which the picture is formed by cubes or square shapes.

culvert (kul´ vərt) *n.* A large drain pipe that goes under a road.

curtsy (kûrt´ sē) *n.* A greeting in which women and girls bend the knees and lower the body.

dahlia (dal´ yə) *n.* A plant with showy, bright-colored flowers.

dangle (dang´ gəl) *v.* To hang down loosely.

debris (də brē´) *n.* Rubbish; trash.

deceive (di sēv´) *v.* To trick; to cheat.

depression (di presh´ ən) *n.* A shallow hole or a dent.

despite (di spīt´) *prep.* In spite of; regardless of.

deter (di tûr´) *v.* To hold back; to prevent.

discard (di skärd´) *v.* To throw away.

disgrace (dis grās´) *v.* To act badly; to shame.

dismay (dis mā´) *n.* A feeling of being discouraged.

dispute (di spyoot´) *v.* To argue; to quarrel.

dither (dith´ ər) *n.* An upset, confused feeling.

dollop (dol´ əp) *n.* A blob of something; a small amount of something.

dweller (dwel´ ər) *n.* Someone who lives in a certain place.

dwelling (dwel´ ing) *n.* A place to live.

E

encounter (en koun´ tər) *v.* To meet by chance.

encourage (en kûr´ ij) *v.* To urge or inspire someone to do something.

environment (en vī´ rən mənt) *n.* Everything surrounding a plant, animal, or person.

exhaust (ig zôst´) *n.* The gases and smoke from a car that go into the air.

exploration (ek´ splə rā´ shən) *n.* The act of searching or looking closely at a new area.

extraordinary (ik strôr´ dn er´ ē) *adj.* Rare; not ordinary.

F

falcon (fôl´ kən) *n.* A powerful bird of prey.

faze (fāz) *v.* To bother.

flat (flat) *n.* A musical note that sounds one-half tone lower than it usually does.

flatter (flat´ ər) *adj.* More flat.

flimsy (flim´ zē) *adj.* Weak; slight; breakable.

florist (flor´ ist) *n.* A person who sells flowers.

flourish (flûr´ ish) *v.* To grow well; to succeed.

ford (ford) *v.* To cross a river or stream.

forecast (for´ kast´) *v.* To tell what will happen.

forefeet (for´ fēt´) *n.* Plural of **forefoot:** One of the front feet of a four-legged animal.

fragrant (frā´ grənt) *adj.* Sweet-smelling.

fugitive (fyoo´ ji tiv) *n.* A person or animal who runs away.

G

gamble (gam´ bəl) *n.* A risk; a chance.

gnarled (närld) *adj.* Full of twists and bumps; knotted.

Gothic (goth´ ik) *adj.* A style of art that uses much detail and decoration.

greasewood (grēs´ wood´) *n.* A woody plant that grows in the dry West.

greenhouse (grēn´ hous´) *n.* A building for growing plants.

grim (grim) *adj.* Stern; harsh.

grope (grōp) *v.* To seek or feel blindly.

gutter (gut´ ər) *n.* A curved path or trough for carrying off rainwater.

> **Pronunciation Key: at**; l**ā**te; c**â**re; f**ä**ther; s**e**t; m**ē**; **i**t; k**ī**te; **o**x; r**ō**se; **ô** in b**ou**ght; c**oi**n; b**ōō**k; t**ōō**; f**o**rm; **ou**t; **u**p; **u**se; t**û**rn; **ə** sound in **a**bout, chick**e**n, penc**i**l, cann**o**n, circ**u**s; **ch**air; **hw** in **wh**ich; ri**ng**; **sh**op; **th**in; **tH**ere; **zh** in trea**s**ure.

H

habitat (hab′ i tat′) *n.* The natural surroundings of a plant or animal.

haunch (hônch) *n.* The hip and the thickest part of the thigh.

hearth (härth) *n.* The floor of a fireplace.

hedge (hej) *n.* A row of bushes used as a fence.

hesitate (hez′ i tāt′) *v.* To pause; to be unsure.

hinge (hinj) *n.* A metal joint that attaches a door to its frame and lets the door move.

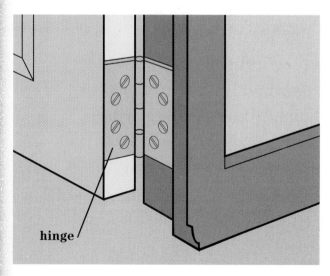

hinge

hoa-phuong (hwä fung) *n.* *Vietnamese.* A tropical flower in Vietnam that has groups of red blossoms.

hostility (ho stil′ i tē) *n.* Unfriendliness; willingness to fight.

hover (huv′ ər) *v.* To hang in the air near something.

humiliation (hyōō mil′ ē ā′ shən) *n.* An action or event that hurts someone's pride.

I

imagination (i maj′ ə nā′ shən) *n.* The ability to create new ideas in one's mind.

imitate (im′ i tāt′) *v.* To copy.

immature (im′ ə chōōr′) *adj.* Not fully grown.

imprint (im′ print) *n.* A mark made by something pressing.

inclined (in klīnd′) *adj.* Usually wants to do something.

Indostan (in′ də stan) *n.* An old-time name for India and Pakistan combined.

initially (i nish′ əl lē) *adv.* At first.

intersection (in′ tər sek′ shən) *n.* The place where two streets cross each other.

intruder (in trōō′ dər) *n.* Someone who enters a place against the owner's will.

island (ī′ lənd) *n.* 1. A piece of land surrounded by water. 2. Anything surrounded by something else.

intimidate (in tim′ i dāt′) *v.* To threaten; to try to scare.

J

jangle (jang′ gəl) *v.* To make a harsh sound, like two pieces of metal hitting each other.

jiggle (jig′ əl) *v.* To move back and forth quickly.

jostle (jos′ əl) *v.* To bump into.

K

kip (kip) *n.* A nap; sleep.

L

launch (lônch) *v.* To begin.

lifespan (līf′ span′) *n.* The amount of time a thing lives.

limply (limp′ lē) *adv.* Loosely.

lollop (lä′ ləp) *v.* To move in a slow, lazy way.

lope (lōp) *v.* To take long steps while running.

lunge (lunj) *v.* To leap forward at someone or something.

lurk (lûrk) *v.* To hide.

lush (lush) *adj.* Fresh; tender; abundant.

lute (lŏŏt) *n.* An old-time string instrument with a pear shape and a bent neck, played by plucking its strings.

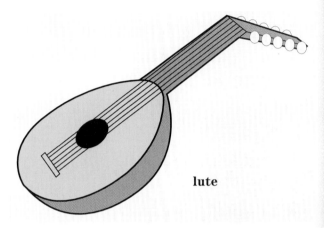

lute

luxury (luk′ shə rē) *n.* Anything a person cannot afford.

M

margin (mär′ jin) *n.* The blank edge of a paper.

marvel (mär′ vəl) *n.* A wonderful or amazing thing.

matchless (mach′ lis) *adj.* The best.

metallic (mə tal′ ik) *adj.* As if made of metal.

micky (mik′ ē) *n.* A potato.

microscope (mī′ krə skōp′) *n.* An instrument that makes small things look larger.

migrate (mī´ grāt) *v.* To move
from colder to warmer lands and
back again.

miniature (min´ē ə chər) *adj.* Tiny;
very small.

miserable (miz´ ər ə bəl) *adj.* Very
unhappy.

molt (mōlt) *v.* To drop off feathers.

monument (mon´ yə mənt) *n.*
Anything built to honor a person
or event.

monument

mortar (mor´ tər) *n.* A mixture like
cement used to hold bricks
together.

mottled (mot´ ld) *adj.* Spotted or
blotched with different colors.

mound (mound) *n.* A pile or heap
of something.

mustache (mus´ tash) *n.* Hair
grown on the upper lip.

musty (mus´ tē) *adj.* Stale; moldy.

N

nestling (nest´ ling) *n.* A bird too
young to leave the nest.

newsstand (nooz´ stand´) *n.* An
outdoor booth where newspapers
are sold.

nonstop (non´ stop´) *adv.*
Constantly; all the time.

nook (nook) *n.* A small, hidden
place.

notion (nō´ shən) *n.* An idea.

nudge (nuj) *v.* To push; to poke.

O

observant (əb zûr´ vənt) *adj.*
Watchful; careful.

observation (ob´ zûr vā´ shən) *n.*
The act of studying or noticing.

observe (əb zûrv´) *v.* To see; to
look at.

ocotillo (ō´ kə tēl´ yō) *n.* A desert
bush with sharp spines.

opportunity (op´ ər too´ ni tē) *n.*
A good chance.

organization (or´ gə nə zā´ shən) *n.* A group of people who join together for one purpose; a club.

original (ə rij´ ə nl) *adj.* First.

originality (ə rij´ ə nal´ i tē) *n.* Newness; freshness.

originally (ə rij´ ə nl ē) *adv.* At first; in the beginning.

overpass (ō´ vər pas´) *n.* A road that crosses above another road.

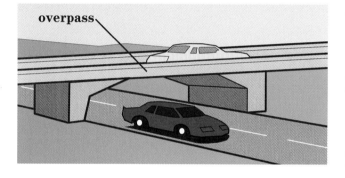
overpass

P

paling (pā´ ling) *n.* A long pointed pole; part of a fence.

parachute (par´ ə shoot´) *n.* An umbrella-shaped object that helps other objects float down slowly from heights.

parasite (par´ ə sīt´) *n.* An animal that lives and feeds on another animal.

particular (pər tik´ yə lər) *adj.* Only; special.

passageway (pas´ ij wā´) *n.* A narrow place to walk between two buildings.

patiently (pā´ shənt lē) *adv.* Without complaining.

peregrine (per´i grin) *n.* A type of falcon that catches other birds in flight.

period (pēr´ ē əd) *n.* An amount of time.

petition (pə tish´ ən) *n.* A written request to someone in charge, signed by those who agree.

petroleum jelly (pe´ trō´ lē əm jel´ ē) *n.* A greasy, sticky substance used to coat things.

plantain (plan´ tin) *n.* A weed that has large leaves and long spikes with small flowers.

plaster (plas´ tər) *n.* A substance like cement that is used to make walls and ceilings.

pollution (pə loo´ shən) *n.* Harmful or dirty material added to the air, water, or soil.

porcupine (por´ kyə pīne) *n.* An animal with stiff pointy hairs.

portion (por´ shən) *n.* A part.

possess (pə zes´) *v.* To have; to own.

prejudice (prej´ ə dis) *n.* Unfairness; an opinion formed without knowing the facts.

prey (prā) *n.* An animal that is hunted to be eaten.

prickly (prik´ lē) *adj.* Full of sharp points that stick or sting.

privet (priv´ it) *n.* A shrub related to the lilac bush and the olive tree. It has small white flowers and smooth, dark fruit; all parts are poisonous.

provoke (prə vōk´) *v.* To cause.

Queen Anne's lace (kwēn´ anz´ lās´) *n.* A wild form of the carrot plant with lacy white flowers.

questioningly (kwes´ chən ing lē) *adv.* In a wondering way.

quill (kwil) *n.* The stiff pointy hairs on a porcupine.

quoth (kwōth) *v. archaic.* Said.

R

rabies (rā´ bēz) *n.* A disease spread by animal bites. Rabies usually causes death unless treated.

racial (rā´ shəl) *adj.* Having to do with a race of people.

rafter (raf´ tər) *n.* One of the beams that hold a roof.

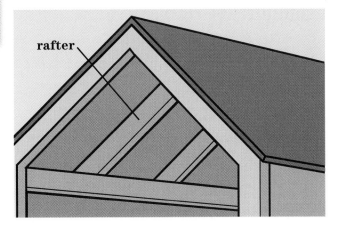

rafter

regardless (ri gärd´ lis) *adv.* Without concern for.

resemble (ri zem´ bəl) *v.* To be like.

respond (ri spond´) *v.* To answer.

responsibility (ri spon´ sə bil´ i tē) *n.* A duty; a job.

rickety (rik´ i tē) *adj.* Shaky; wobbly.

rodent (rōd´ nt) *n.* A type of animal that gnaws with big front teeth. Rodents include mice, rats, beavers, squirrels, and chipmunks.

rogue (rōg) *n.* A person who is not honest; a rascal.

rouse (rouz) *v.* To wake up.

routine (rōō tēn´) *n.* The same actions done over and over.

rubble (rub´ əl) *n.* Rough, broken brick or stone.

S

satisfy (sat´ is fī´) *v.* To fill a need.

scenery (sē´ nə rē) *n.* The painted pictures and objects used on stage in a play.

scope (skōp) *n.* The amount of space.

scrawl (skrôl) *v.* To write in a fast, messy way. —*n.* A scribble.

sculpt (skulpt) *v.* To make a figure, statue, or design by carving wood or stone or by forming clay.

sculpture (skulp´ chər) *n.* A figure, statue, or design carved out of something solid.

segregation (seg´ ri gā´ shən) *n.* Keeping different races of people apart from each other.

seize (sēz) *v.* To grasp; to grab.

seldom (sel´ dəm) *adv.* Rarely; not often.

selfish (sel´ fish) *adj.* Caring only about oneself; not caring about others.

sensitive (sen´ si tiv) *adj.* Able to feel things well.

serenade (ser´ ə nād´) *n.* Music sung to someone.

sesame (ses´ə mē) *n.* The seed of an Asian plant which is used to add flavor to food.

sewer (sōō´ ər) *n.* An underground pipe that carries dirty water away from buildings.

shades (shādz) *n.* Sunglasses.

sharp (shärp) *n.* A musical note that sounds one-half tone higher than it usually does. —*adj.* 1. Clear. 2. Keen.

shock (shok) *v.* To surprise and upset at the same time.

shutter (shut´ ər) *n.* A doorlike cover that opens and closes over a window.

shutter

soar (sor) *v.* To fly at a great height.

sought (sôt) *v.* Past tense of **seek:** To look for.

spake (spāk) *v.* An old-fashioned past tense of **speak:** To talk.

species (spē´ shēz) *n.* An animal family; a kind of animal.

splinter (splin´ tər) *n.* A small sharp piece of wood broken off from a larger piece.

squeegee (skwē´ jē) *v.* To make a squeaking sound by rubbing as if using a squeegee, which is a rubber-edged tool for removing excess water from windows.

squiggle (skwig´ əl) *n.* A line that is curved or wavy.

squirm (skwûrm) *v.* To wriggle.

stalk (stôk) *n.* The stem of a plant.

starve (stärv) *v.* To die from hunger.

statue (stach´ oo) *n.* A carved figure of a person or an animal.

sternly (stûrn´ lē) *adv.* In a strict or harsh way.

stoop (stoop) *n.* A small porch.

stout (stout) *adj.* Sturdy; strong.

strewn (stroon) *v.* A past tense of **strew:** To scatter; to spread around.

stucco (stuk´ ō) *n.* Plaster that covers outside walls.

style (stīl) *n.* The way something is done.

suburb (sub´ ûrb) *n.* A town on the outer edge of a larger city.

suggestion (səg jes´ chən) *n.* An idea; advice.

suitable (soo´ tə bəl) *adj.* Fitting; right.

sycamore (sik´ ə mor´) *n.* A shade tree; a buttonwood tree.

T

taunt (tônt) *n.* Spoken words that make fun of someone in a mean way.

temperature (tem´ pər ə chər) *n.* The hotness or coldness of a thing.

terror (ter´ ər) *n.* Great fear.

theoretically (thē´ ə ret´ i klē) *adv.* According to ideas; supposedly; in the mind.

thresh (thresh) *v.* To throw oneself about wildly; to thrash.

thus (thus) *adv.* In this way.

torrent (tor´ ənt) *n.* A swiftly rushing stream of water.

treachery (trech´ ə rē) *n.* Betrayal; trickery.

trestle (tres´ əl) *n.* A framework that holds up train tracks above a river or above the ground.

trestle

trill (tril) *v.* To make a vibrating sound, like the sound some birds make.

tundra (tun´ drə) *n.* In the arctic regions, a flat plain with no trees.

tusk (tusk) *n.* A long, curving tooth or fang.

typical (tip´ i kəl) *adj.* Usual.

U

urban (ûr´ bən) *adj.* In a city.

V

vacant (vā´ kənt) *adj.* Empty.

ventilation (ven´ tl ā´ shən) *n.* The process of bringing in fresh air.

vigilante (vij´ ə lan´ tē) *n.* A person who acts as if he or she is the law.

violently (vī´ ə lənt lē) *adv.* With destructive force.

visible (viz´ ə bəl) *adj.* Able to be seen.

W

wart hog (wort´ hôg´) *n.* An African wild pig.

wharves (hworvz) *n.* Plural of **wharf:** A pier at which ships stop.

whine (hwīn) *v.* To talk in a complaining, annoying voice.

wholesaler (hōl´ sāl´ ər) *n.* A business that sells to stores.

wilt (wilt) *v.* To become limp; droop.

windowsill (win´ dō sil´) *n.* The flat piece of wood at the bottom of a window.

windswept (wind´ swept´) *adj.* Blown by wind constantly.

wondrous (wun´ drəs) *adj.* Rare; surprising.

worthwhile (wûrth´ hwīl´) *adj.* Important enough to do; rewarding.

Z

zoologist (zō ol´ ə jist) *n.* A person who studies animals.

Unit Opening Art
Unit 1 (Friendship) Sylvie Wickstrom
Unit 2 (City Wildlife) Ed Miller
Unit 3 (Imagination) Jon Agee

Photo Credits